KABINI ON MY MIND

Musings of a Naturalist

VIKRAM NANJAPPA

ISBN
Hardcase 979-8-89544-583-9
Paperback 979-8-89475-978-4

To my relatives and other animals

Illustrations: Alok Ranjan
Editing: Preanka Roy
Encouragement: Gowri & Tara Nanjappa
Compassion & Understanding: Scotty Nanjappa

CONTENTS

MEETING MY WILD SIDE

In the winter of 2002-03 I found myself in Kabini managing a farmhouse that was taking its first baby steps towards becoming a wildlife resort and if you had asked me a year earlier if that was where I saw myself a year hence, I would have laughed in your face. As the 1900s turned to the 2000s I was happily living on the Bhutan border, managing a tea estate and indulging in my love of photography and wildlife.

I did not know then that the previously dreaded but now forgotten Y2K problem would culminate in me reaching Kabini in the middle of the night to discover that my quarters had an outdoor toilet without a door. Not wishing to make a fuss, I decided to tackle the problem in the morning by catching the first available transport out. As day broke and I got my first look ... the rest, as they say, is history.

I was shortly joined by my wife Gowri, my daughter Tara and our dog (a St Bernard mix) Bernie. We later added another member to our family – Bruno, a dachshund. In Kabini I eagerly embarked on the next phase of my wildlife journey, exploring the forests and honing my skills as a Naturalist. Up until then I had been happily engrossed in tackling the human-elephant conflict prevailing in the Duars and keeping track of the resident leopards on the estate. I enjoyed my wild life in the Duars, observing elephants and, to a lesser degree, leopards.

We stayed in Kabini for nearly ten years, finally leaving in 2011 by when I had become the Chief Naturalist at Evolve Back, and Kabini had become one of the premier wildlife destinations in India.

KABINI: THE MOTHER RIVER

While Kabini is a well-known destination among the wildlife lovers in India, I feel that a few clarifications are in order. There seems to be a common misunderstanding among people and a lot of them use terms like 'Kabini forest', 'Kabini National Park' and 'Kabini Tiger Reserve' when referring to the area. Kabini is not a separate protected area but a part of the Nagarhole National Park, which to add to the confusion, is also known as the Rajiv Gandhi National Park. Nagarhole spans the Mysore and Coorg districts of Karnataka and has two tourism zones where game viewing by tourists is permitted. On the south-western side of the Park lies the Sunkadakatte Tourism Zone which includes a stretch of the Kabini River.

It is this zone that tourists are familiar with and is casually referred to as 'Kabini' by them. Safaris or game drives are organised by the resorts located there. Two drives, of approximately three hours each, are allowed daily. One in the morning and one in the evening, no tourism is permitted during the rest of the day.

The Kabini river, also known as Kapila, originates in the Wayanad district of Kerala and is formed by the confluence of the Panamaram and Mananthavady rivers. It flows eastwards into Karnataka and joins the Kaveri River at Tirumakudalu Narasipura.

While it flows through three Protected Areas, the casual visitor or tourist can only access it from the Nagarhole National Park side. Our Protected Areas are divided into zones namely Buffer, Tourism and Core, with the Tourism Zone being the only one open to the public.

The Sunkadakatte Tourism Zone is representative of the forest types of the region with a mix of dry and moist deciduous forests and includes the famed backwaters of the Kabini which is a unique micro-habitat on its own. This zone is located in the DB Kuppe and Antarasante Wildlife Ranges. As this is a tourism area certain measures have been taken to facilitate wildlife viewing here.

These include a good network of game roads which enable the tourists to cover all the forest types in the region. About thirty metres on both sides of the roads have been cleared of undergrowth to improve visibility. A large number of artificial salt licks are maintained by the Forest Department all along these roads to attract herds of herbivores.

The Department has also created waterholes close to these roads. Some of these are Bisalwadi, KV Tank and Tiger Tank (so named due to the frequent sightings of the famous felines spotted here) have watchtowers. The Bisalwadi Watchtower is usually available for viewing during the game drive (rules governing the use of watchtowers are subject to change and it's best to check beforehand), but it can get quite crowded at times which usually takes away from the experience. All this makes this zone an excellent place for viewing wildlife.

The area called the Russell Line, named after a British Forest Officer, is representative of the dry deciduous type of forest where the Axle Wood Tree (Anogeissus latifolia) dominates the landscape. The wood of this tree used to be used in the construction of bullock carts and agricultural implements hence the common name. The undergrowth here is sparser than the other areas of the Tourism Zone. A waterhole called the Nainji Katte is located here. It tends to dry up during the summer.

This is the only place within the Tourism Zone that includes the habitat favoured by the Four — Horned Antelope, the only species of antelope in Nagarhole, unfortunately it is very rarely seen. Due to the extremely dry nature of the forest here, safari vehicles tend to neglect the area. However this area is a personal favourite and is highly recommended as it gives the discerning visitor a feel of a dry deciduous forest. Close to the Russell Line is the Temple Road, so called because it passes an old tribal temple. This road leads to the GK Tank (waterhole).

Further north, past the Bisalwadi waterhole, is the Kymara road that takes you to the Bar Balle area which is representative of the moist deciduous forest type and is dominated by tree species like Teak (Tectona grandis) and Nandi (Lagrestreomia lanceolata). Being a higher rainfall area, the trees here are larger and taller than in the dry deciduous areas. The undergrowth is also much denser.

The terrain here is also very different from the rest of the Tourism Zone, being a little hilly in nature. The game roads follow the course of the Balle River, a rain-fed stream that is a tributary of the Kabini. At one point a check dam has been built across the Balle River. This is a good spot to stop and watch wildlife.

There is a high-tension power line that cuts across this part of the Tourism Zone, starting from the Mysore-Mananthavady Road and proceeds north towards Kerala. There is a game road that runs alongside, commonly referred to as the 'Power Line'. If one drives the entire length of this road one can experience the gradual change in forest type from dry to moist deciduous. Sections of this road are favoured by the Naturalists from the lodges, especially the section between the Tiger Tank and the road leading to the KV Tank for their excellent wildlife viewing opportunities.

The backwaters of the Kabini need no introduction. This area of the Tourism Zone contains extensive teak plantations that were raised by felling large areas; this practice has now fortunately been stopped. The area falls within the moist zone and contains good specimens of Rosewood (Dalbergia latifolia), the stately Yellow Teak (Adena cordifolia), the Crocodile Bark Tree (Terminalia tomentosa) and members of the Ficus family. During the summer, when the water levels recede, it turns into a vast grassland and wildlife viewing at that time is more akin to Africa than India.

This grassland plays host to one of the largest congregations of Asiatic elephants in the world. It is also at this time when the Mastigudi temple emerges from the receding waters. The old Kakankote State Forest, the venue of the famous Mysore Kheddas, borders this area. Driving along the banks is not allowed as it disturbs the wildlife, especially the elephants. Nevertheless there are certain points along the backwaters where one can stop the vehicle and enjoy spectacular wildlife scenes.

The Sunset Point offers probably the best panoramic view of the backwaters with the setting sun in the background. This is the best place to end an evening safari. Other places of note along the backwaters are Boating Point or Mastigudi, the President's Road, the Nilgiri Plantation and the Old MM Road. The Kumbalavali Road is in many ways similar to Bar Balle, with undulating terrain and large trees.

Taking a safari in Kabini is an exhilarating experience if done properly. To fully enjoy and experience nature the visitor needs to be extremely sensitive to his surroundings and display a large measure of patience and self-discipline. A safari can be best described as a sojourn into the wild and there are many ways to do so. Most parks in India, Kabini included, offer Jeep rides into the park and these are one of the best ways to safari.

The advantage of a Jeep ride is that one is able to cover a lot of ground in the shortest possible time thus maximising one's chances of encountering wildlife. However most Jeep safaris turn out to be just mindless driving in the forest. One needs to stop every now and then, especially near ecological features, like waterholes, that attract wildlife. A discerning guide is necessary on any safari and he should not be pressured to show animals, as no one is a magician to be able to conjure up wildlife. Sounds play an important role and one must be willing to stop and spend time listening.

In my opinion the best way to view wildlife in Kabini, especially during the dry season, is by boat. Boat safaris are conducted both in the morning and evening. During the dry season, water is let out for irrigation and the lake dries out leaving only the main river visible. Many small islands are formed and petrified trees rise out of the waters giving a surreal effect to the entire landscape. These temporary islands are favoured by both crocodiles and elephants.

The fresh succulent grass on these islands attracts the elephants and it is common to sight these magnificent animals swimming across the river to get to them. These islands become the exclusive preserve of the elephants as no other herbivore can gain access to them. However, the elephants have competition from an unlikely source — River Terns. These birds build their nests on the ground and are always wary of getting trampled by elephants. It is common to spot a large number of these birds mobbing the elephants and driving them away from the islands.

Trekking in protected areas is discouraged in India and Kabini is no exception. The average tourist does not possess the skills required to survive in the forest and is thus most vulnerable while on foot. Fitness levels and the ability to climb trees plays an important role in escaping danger while on foot but as these are hard to assess it is best to avoid going into the forest on foot.

Most lodges offer Nature Walks or Birdwatching walks which are conducted both within their well-wooded premises, along the river bank (outside the Park) and through agricultural fields. These are greatly rewarding experiences especially for avid birdwatchers and are highly recommended. If you are a keen birdwatcher I strongly recommend you ask the resort's Naturalist to allow you to indulge in a night walk in and around the property as there are extremely good chances of spotting owls and other nocturnal species like nightjars.

Kabini is rated as one of the best wildlife destinations in India and ranks extremely high on the 'To do List' of both the domestic and international traveller. However a note of caution is in order — Kabini can be highly addictive.

This book is a compilation of various musings, natural history notes, opinions and incidents that occurred in Kabini during my stint there. While they are arranged in no particular order, they were written as they occurred (I maintained an online journal at the time) and accurately reflect my mood, opinions and emotions as the incidents played out. A lot of water has flowed by since but I have resisted the temptation to 'update' them as I feel hindsight is not always a good thing – it can be unfair to those who actually lived through the moment.

COOLING EFFECT

The Ficus trees are now fruiting, and during this season of scarcity, they become one of the best places to view wildlife. Not only does the fruit attract many animals and birds, but the thick canopy of these trees provides much-needed shade in the hot months when almost every other tree is leafless.

I spent some time under one of these trees the other day. This one was near the old Mysore-Malabar road, and I was able to park my Jeep right under the tree. At first I speculated that this tree must have been planted years ago when the road was made, as Ficus trees used to be planted along roads in the old days. Many of these old trees were ruthlessly cut down during the road widening work carried out on the stretch of the same road outside the park last year. It is a pity that we destroy our green cover in the name of development.

The first thing I noticed was the drop in temperature under the tree; it was at least four or five degrees cooler. I was not alone and a herd of chital was also foraging under the dry leaf litter beneath the tree.

The noise levels were extremely high as a large number of common and hill mynas were busy on the upper branches of the tree. Troops of langur were also busy feasting on the fruit. They were dropping a large number on the ground, which was what the chital were looking for under the leaf litter.

I spent a pleasant half-hour listening to the sounds and enjoying the activity under the tree. I did not indulge in any birdwatching as

I wanted to take in the bigger picture. However, I heard, besides the mynas, the plum-headed parakeets, imperial green pigeons, the ever-present and noisy Jungle Babblers and a Racquet-tailed drongo, all of them in or around the tree.

Visitors to Kabini come to spend some time in the wild and to take in the serene atmosphere. They especially enjoy an idyllic safari, and most of them go home with a very sentimental picture of the wild. Those of us who live and work here are aware that things are not so simple.

Take death, for instance. Whenever a tiger dies, there is a hue and cry on social media and in the news. But death is in the natural order of things. However unnatural deaths caused by humans are another matter.

One of the most insidious and silent killers are fishing nets. People entering the Park illegally put out these fishing nets, and many of them get snagged in the petrified tree stumps and become a nuisance to wildlife. It may be surprising to know that a fishing net can kill such large animals, but I have seen large crocodiles killed by these nets.

The Forest Department needs to take this seriously right now, as we see fishermen operating within the Park with impunity. They brazenly go about their business in their coracles right in front of us, making no attempt to hide. So much for the oft-repeated argument that wildlife tourism acts as a watchdog against poaching.

Yesterday during the evening boat safari, we noticed something flapping against a stump. It turned out to be a Black-rumped flameback that had gotten trapped in an old fishing net.

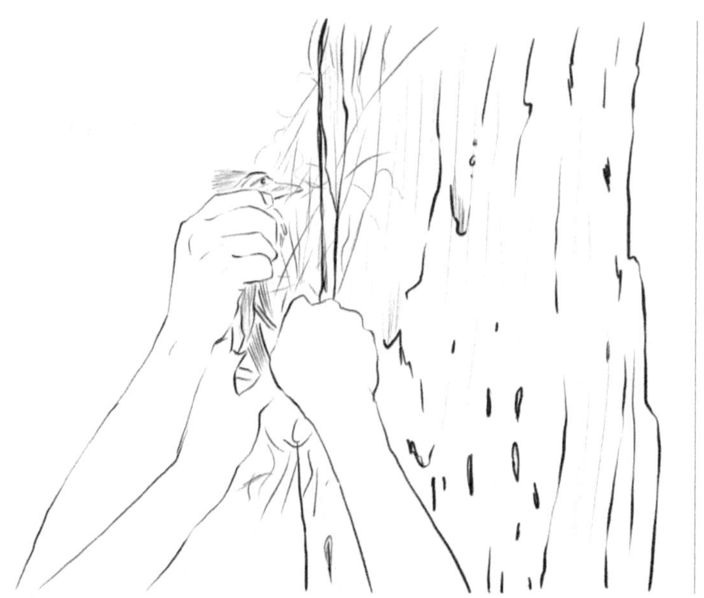

While the damage done to birds is less noticeable, many water birds fall victim to these nets. Luckily for this particular bird we were able to notice and rescue him; otherwise, he would have died of hunger and exhaustion. I have even seen a darter unable to open its mouth because it was jammed shut by a fishing net. I was unable to get to it, and I shuddered at how it might have died, slowly starving to death.

Unfortunately, a few days ago, we arrived too late to save an Indian Rock Python. Pythons like to swim, and this one swam right into a net and could not get out. A python is a rare sight in Kabini, and a dead one was a sad sight indeed. The other day, I got a sinking feeling when I came across a dead gaur floating in the water. I have no idea how it died, but I couldn't help but fear the worst.

One morning, my friend Nawaraj witnessed a bizarre scene in the backwaters: an elephant (a tusker) entangled in a fishing net. He must have got entangled while swimming over.

Fortunately the tusker managed to free himself; I could not quite fathom how the Forest Department personnel would have tackled this problem. The ending may not have been so happy if a young calf had been caught in deep water. It just goes to show the damage fishing with nets can do in wildlife areas. All of us who feel that fishing is non-intrusive and can be allowed in wildlife areas as a dual-use policy need to give it a good thought.

On my part I managed to get these incidents highlighted (along with photographic evidence) through an article in the local press. How effective that was is anybody's guess.

KARAPURA TIGRESS

For the past six months, a tiger has strayed out of the Park and is often seen frequenting the Karapura Village. It is usually seen in the late evenings, and while it has taken a toll on the village cattle, the tiger has never harmed anyone.

Yesterday evening, the Forest Department finally managed to tranquilise it. The tigress (it turned out to be a young tigress) was taken to the Sunkadakatte Forest Rest House for safekeeping as it was feared that the villagers might try and kill it. The killing of trapped predators has occurred in various parts of India, and securing its safety after capture has become a priority.

During yesterday's evening safari, I visited the Forest Rest House and saw the trapped tigress for myself. She still looked a little under the influence of the drug and had left her food untouched. After making a few inquiries, I learned that they still had not decided what to do with her.

After much deliberation within the department and with various tiger biologists, it was finally decided that she should be released into the Bhadra WLS.

I was of the opinion that the Forest Department had made the right choice, as Bhadra has a reasonably decent prey base but not a healthy tiger population. It is also well protected. It was the perfect place for her, and she would have also invigorated the Bhadra tiger gene pool.

Unfortunately, it was not to be, as, after a week or so, she was found dead. It appears that she died of fatigue and starvation.

While the Forest Department estimated her age to be six years, I felt that she was probably three. If she was six years old, she should have been a breeding resident with her own cubs. Breeding females usually acquire stable home ranges and start breeding at three to four years of age. They usually manage to hold on to their range for about five to seven years and produce litters of three to four cubs once every two to three years. It is highly unlikely for a six-year-old tigress to be pushed out of her home range or for a tigress of that age not to have established a range of her own. That is one more reason why I felt that the Forest Department had got her age wrong.

In my opinion, she was a young female who had recently become independent of her mother and was trying to carve out a territory of her own. Not finding enough space in the Park due to the prevailing high density of tigers, she was compelled to wander out and tried to establish herself near the village where she lived off cattle. We knew she was there for the past seven months. This is a common occurrence in places with healthy tiger populations like Nagarhole.

I speculate that as she had gotten used to lifting cattle, which is very easy, she may not have been able to hunt wild prey effectively, hence her death. It was also possible she was already malnourished when captured due to the lack of a proper diet (there had not been too many cattle kills in the village). I only hope that the effects of tranquilisation or the sedatives administered during transportation had not compounded her problems.

MISSED OPPORTUNITY

A few days ago, I missed an opportunity to spend a night in the Park and that too on the water. I set out for a safari as usual with a boatload of people at 4:30 pm, and there was nothing exceptional about the safari as we slowly drifted along. At around 5:30 pm, I was getting a bit worried as we had not seen much wildlife when I spotted an elephant on the opposite bank browsing on some bamboo beside the water. I decided to get a little closer as I could feel that the guests were a bit listless, and I thought that the elephants would lift their spirits.

As we were getting across, bang in the middle of the river, the boat hit a submerged tree stump. Now, that is putting it mildly — the boat had been rocked pretty badly on impact, and the stump had drilled a hole one and a half feet in diameter and about nine inches deep into the bottom of the boat. As luck would have, it was a hardwood tree and try as we could, we could not free the boat — we were stuck on that stump in the middle of the river.

My first duty was to ensure that the guests, who were panicking by now, were sent back to the resort as soon as possible. Luckily, another boat was passing by, and they took our guests on board. I then informed the resort by radio to come and get me. That done, I settled down for a long wait.

The setting was beautiful, and I began to relax. Slowly, as the evening progressed and the light started to fade, I began to doze off, only to be awakened by the roar of a tiger. Both Shivraj, my boatman, and I heard it clearly. Now, a tiger's roar is not an ear-splitting one; if you don't know what to expect, you can miss it entirely. Anyway, that woke us up, and we started scanning the river bank with our binoculars. It was still light enough to make out a tiger if it appeared.

After five minutes, bonnet macaques started alarm calling, and we were able to track the tiger's progress by their calls and the alarm calls of the langur, spotted deer and a Malabar Giant Squirrel, who joined in. Each called out as the tiger came within their sight. All this took up the better part of an hour until the alarm calls of sambar, far off in the distance and away from the banks, confirmed that the tiger had moved on.

We then settled down again and watched the moon and the stars reflected on the river. It was now well past 9 pm when we heard the rescue boat approaching us. To cut a long story short, we were unable to dislodge the boat—it continued to pivot around the stump. We then called for another boat, and even when that arrived, we were unable to get our boat out.

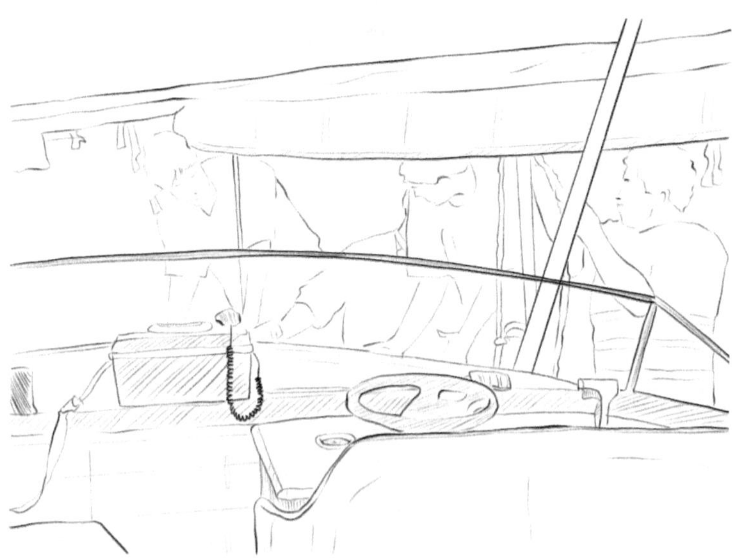

This was precisely what I was hoping for, and I told the General Manager (Jain Kumar) that I would stay back in the boat and that he could return the next day along with the equipment required to lift the boat. He reluctantly agreed and started to move away when he suddenly decided to give it one last try. As luck would have it, the damn boat came loose, and we were able to head home. It was past 1 am when we reached the resort, and driving back in the middle of the night in pitch darkness was great fun.

LIGHTS IN THE NIGHT

People who live around the wilderness know the effects of light pollution on the movements and habits of nocturnal wildlife. Resorts and hotels coming up in these areas are also becoming sensitive to this issue and are taking care to ensure that public lighting is subdued, well-designed, and non-polluting.

Public roads running through Protected Areas are being closed to traffic during the night to reduce the disturbance to wildlife. Night safaris are not allowed in any National Park or Protected Area in India. All safaris end at dusk and only begin after daybreak, with the afternoons being kept free from tourism. The idea is to make tourism as unobtrusive as possible.

When hunting was legal in the past, it was governed by strict rules and codes of conduct. Wilderness areas were still difficult to access, and hunting was by no means free from danger or excitement. Acquiring a fine trophy was no easy task. Besides it took great planning, logistics, and days of hard trekking to reach the hunting blocks.

All this changed with the arrival of the motorcar. Suddenly roads sprang up all over the place, and most forests, save the real remote ones, became accessible to the casual traveller who owned a motorcar. This led to a general spurt in hunting, and genuine hunters of the old school, who were also conservationists in their own way, were appalled and warned that easy access was diminishing India's wildlife at an alarming rate.

The arrival of better guns and spotlights was the next step. Now all the 'hunter' had to do was drive along a forest road safe and sound in his car. Point his spotlight all around and blast away at any pair of eyes that reflected back. Most of the time, the bright light would disorient and immobilise the animal, making it a sitting duck.

I firmly believe that today's wildlife photographers are the modern avatars of the hunters of the old days. Both were driven by their love of wildlife, their skill and mastery over their equipment, the thrill of the chase and the final acquisition of a fine trophy. I am a wildlife photographer, and I can state quite categorically that if I had been born two generations ago, I would have been a big game hunter. In fact, it was my childhood dream to be a big game hunter in Africa.

Unfortunately, wildlife photographers can also be divided into ethical and unethical ones. And it is also not surprising that the ethics of wildlife photography almost mirror those of hunting. In fact the rules, regulations, ethics and traditions of hunting are much stricter than that of wildlife photography and also, in my considered opinion, led to a closer relationship between the hunter and the pursued. There was genuine respect for the hunt and wildlife, and it comes as no surprise that the first conservationists (as we know them today) were hunters.

This brings me to the question, what do you make of a wildlife photographer who drives along forest roads in the night with a spotlight and uses a flash to take photographs? Is there any difference between him and the unethical hunter of the old days? True, the end result is only a photograph and not the death of the animal, but is it not intrusive? In this day and age, and taking into consideration the background given above, can it be considered ethical?

These days, I get a strong feeling that I belong to another era; is that era in the past or future? I am not too sure. Recently, after seeing a photograph of a tiger (taken in exactly the same circumstances mentioned as unethical above) I put up this same question for discussion on the forum of the photo-sharing website on which the photograph appeared. I was looking forward to a healthy debate and exchange of views instead of which I found that the moderators chose to remove my post. Are we afraid to question ourselves, or are some people so infallible that they can be considered beyond criticism?

SNAKES NOT SNACKS

Any rural roadside hotel worth its name, or for that matter, even some in metropolitan areas in India, have a habit of serving 'snakes'. Don't be alarmed, what they actually mean is 'snacks'. As I see it, English is an odd language, and anybody attempting to master its spellings, especially if they came to it later in life, is probably going to get more than they bargained for. Fortunately, we don't fall in the same category, but be warned that if you see such a sign at Kabini — it will mean exactly what it says! We have snakes here, and though we don't serve them, we are extremely proud of them. Let me introduce you to a few.

Flying Snakes

An Ornate Flying Snake was found on the wall of one of the rooms the other day. The snake was found by the Housekeeping Department and they immediately called me up. The creature was long, slender, smooth-scaled, mildly venomous, and 'ornate' as it sported black cross-hatching and yellow or gold-coloured accents.

These snakes are diurnal, and though arboreal, can sometimes be seen on low bushes or in grass. It is an uncommon snake, and I was surprised and delighted to see one. However, despite its name, it does not fly. It glides by extending its ribs and pulling in the underside. It virtually swims through the air and can glide a distance of a hundred meters. It also climbs well, aided by notched angular belly scales. While I was taking a few photographs, it suddenly took off from the wall and disappeared in a flash. The housekeeping boys who were watching were amazed. They thought it was magic.

The Wine List

The next snake that was 'served up' was the Common Vine Snake. Despite its name, it's not a snack that is served with wine but a snake in its own right. Though I must admit its spelling opens up a host of possibilities. It's a blessing that our roadside eateries are unaware of it. Can you imagine the sign "Warning — Common Wine Snacks!" at a hotel?

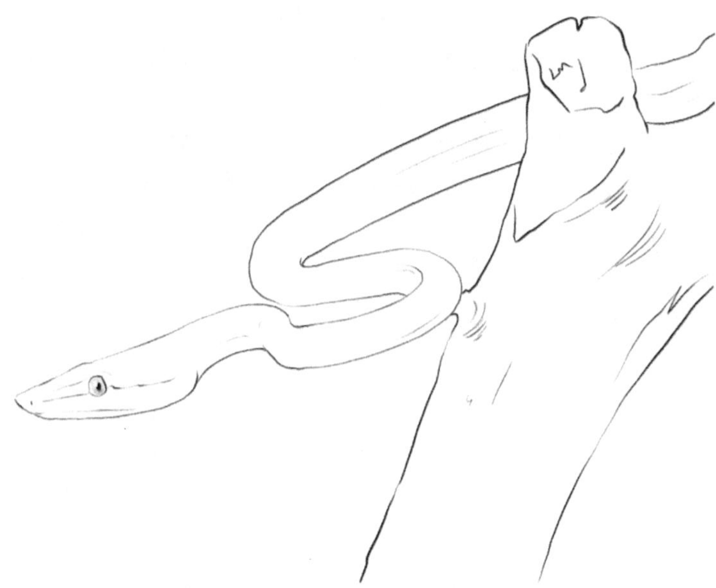

True to its name, it is quite common here and also does look like a vine on a bush or tree; I guess that's why it's called a Vine Snake. The Common Vine Snake is a long, slender, smooth-scaled snake with an extremely pointed head and has an extended snout, and large eyes with horizontal pupils. It also has a long tail. In fact, everything about it seems to be long. It is diurnal, that is, active during the day rather than at night, and is usually seen on low bushes or trees and very rarely on the ground. It feeds mainly on lizards, frogs, small birds, and mice.

One was recorded eating tadpoles, another swallowing a shieldtail snake. In Sri Lanka, it has been seen catching and eating fish. It has mild venom that it uses to paralyse small prey. It has up to twenty-three young ones between March and December.

Blind Snakes

To continue from where we left off, we pride ourselves and rightly so, on the diversity of choice when it comes to our offerings to our guests, and snakes are no exception. However, have you ever heard of a blind snake? Yes, you read that right, I said blind snakes. As you have already met our flying snake, a blind snake should hopefully not come as a surprise.

The thing with blind snakes is that they are very difficult to spot. In fact sometimes I feel that we are the ones that are blind and not them. However there are times when these unexpected visitors turn up quite literally under our own feet, and one day, I spotted one in the area where we conduct tribal dances.

Blind snakes grow up to about 170 mm, have a slender worm-like appearance, and can often be mistaken for earthworms. They live beneath the soil, under stones or debris, and are usually seen only when they are turned over or flushed out of their burrows by rain. They are usually solitary but are occasionally seen in large congregations on rotting wood.

The feared reputation they have is undeserved as they are entirely harmless. They are believed by some to enter the ears of people sleeping on the ground and are hence called *Sevi pamboo* in Tamil. In fact, the poor chaps are preyed upon by other snakes, and in turn, eat larvae, pupae of ants, and other small insects.

The Supermodel

This is a unique specimen and a favourite of mine. I consider her (I always think of them as female, and I am sure that so will you once I finish describing them) the supermodel of Kabini, the showstopper of showstoppers. Beautiful, slender, graceful and like all things beautiful, a joy to watch. I am referring to the Common Bronze-backed Tree Snake. Make no mistake, her beauty is not common.

She is long, slender and her tail is very long and wire-like. She has a snout that is bluntly rounded much like a pout! To top it all off, she has beautiful large eyes. She gets her name from her bronze — brown back. Her runways of choice are low bushes and thorn trees. Extremely agile and fast, she has sharply defined notches on the scales of her belly that help her climb. She can also leap from branch to branch.

Like many supermodels of repute, she has a nervous disposition and a temper to watch out for. Make sure you watch her from a respectable distance as she will strike repeatedly if cornered. However, her bark is worse than her bite — she is non-venomous.

The bronze-back feeds on frogs, garden lizards, geckos, and small birds and the way to her heart is not through fancy shiny baubles but through her stomach. She will willingly enter your home to partake of her favoured delicacies.

Tough Guys

I hope you enjoyed meeting the supermodel of Kabini and while I appreciate all kinds of snakes and people (it takes all sorts to make a world), there are a few types around whom I tend to mind my p's and q's. These are the tough guys, and like most tough guys, they are not really looking for a fight, but one still gives them the respect they command.

Of course, there are always a few young guns among us, who in a vain attempt to prove their manhood take delight in trifling with them. Our stalwarts treat them with disdain preferring not to react unless pushed too far. One such tough guy is the Spectacled Cobra.

This is one of our commoner snakes and is one of the big four among Indian snakes. He is a good swimmer who is usually seen in fields, near streams, rock piles and trees. He often lives in rat holes and termite mounds.

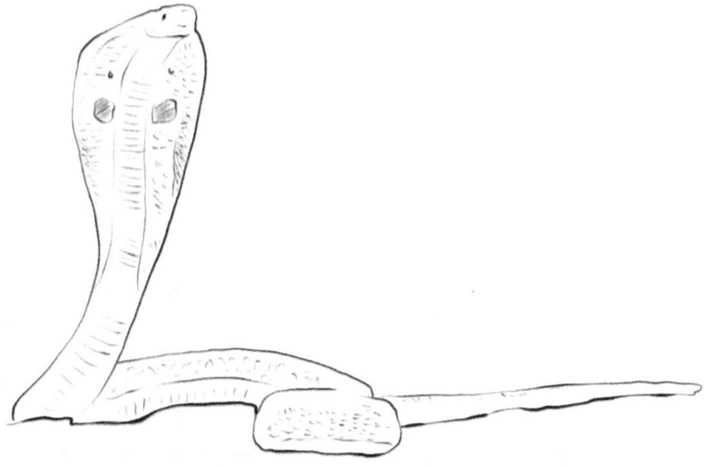

Spectacled cobras are fast and alert snakes, but like most tough guys, they are generally shy but when alarmed, they will raise their fore bodies and spread their hoods. Most of the time, they will limit themselves to this display to convey their message. However, if pushed too far, they will hiss and strike.

Another tough guy who likes to hang around Kabini is the Russell's Viper. Now while his name may suggest that he belongs to someone he is nobody's pet. This tough guy likes to play at night, usually in open grassy areas, scrub jungles, forest edges, rocky hillocks, dense thorny hedgerows and in and around mangroves.

His food of choice happens to be rodents and when disturbed he throws a hissy fit, much like a pressure cooker going off. Though usually slow, he is capable of incredibly fast strikes but only bites as a last resort. One of India's big four medically important snakes, they cause as many, or more, snakebites than cobras. Being heavy-bodied ambush hunters, they are more likely to stand their ground than other venomous snakes. Most people are bitten at night when they step on a viper.

Like most tough guys, these two know that to scare someone is sufficient; the death penalty is for the rarest of rare occasions, and thus though they are responsible for a large number of bites, only a small percentage of these are fatal. Talk of the tough-minded and tender-hearted.

The Wannabe

How many of us have run into people who imitate the mannerisms and the 'look' of a certain type of person to try and pass off as one of them in a vain attempt to fool those around? I am guessing that a lot of us have on numerous occasions bumped into this type. I am also willing to bet that a lot of such people ape the mannerisms of tough guys. Therefore it should come as no surprise that one of the tough guys of

Kabini, whom I introduced in my previous post, the cobra also, has a wannabe. The one in question is the Rat Snake. Apt name one would think, but that's not doing justice to the imposter.

While he looks like a cobra, he certainly is not a rat. Very fast, alert and active, he is a hunter in his own right. He is also a good climber and like the cobra, prefers rat holes and termite mounds as a place to live. He feeds on frogs, toads, lizards, rats, bats, and other snakes, but in a cruel twist of fate, is the preferred food of the king cobra.

He prefers a speedy escape, but when cornered, he will inflate his throat and emit a moan or growl and strike vigorously. However, he is non-poisonous and therefore, incapable of killing us but large individuals can inflict painful but harmless bites. Like most of his ilk, he will quickly calm down when handled gently. Not something I would recommend — snakes like most people are best left alone.

The Dandy

Allow me to introduce you to another unique snake that one can bump into in Kabini. This gentleman is not so easily spotted, and meeting him is a rare privilege. I am one of the privileged few, and I ran into him at the most unexpected of places — near the resort generator shed. What he was doing there is anybody's guess, but then to each his own. The gentleman in question is Elliot's Shieldtail Snake.

The said gent is quite the dandy. However, unlike most dandies, he is a shy creature. He is a small guy, about ten inches long, with a slender body. His scales are smooth and his head is narrower than his neck. To top it all off, his snout is sharply pointed. His rear end is no less interesting. He has a short tail with its tip cut at a slant. The slanted portion is slightly rounded and ends in two small spines. He is glossy dark brown, and sometimes has small yellow dots and sometimes not.

He does, however, have a distinct yellow line along the sides of his neck and a broad yellow stripe on each side of his tail.

The dandy with his fondness for yellow is mostly nocturnal and prefers going about his business at night. He is also an inoffensive burrower with a weakness for earthworms. In fact his diet mainly comprises of them.

THE RESCUE

While one does one's best not to intervene and let nature take its course, we've often been compelled to save or rescue snakes from the resort premises, but this was a different kind of rescue and a first for us.

At about 10 am one morning, I got a frantic call from my wife Gowri, informing me that a bunch of crows were attempting to get at a juvenile Asian Koel, which had, in turn, taken refuge in our garden. Along with Bruno (our dachshund), she was keeping the crows at bay, but she was not sure how long she could hold out and wanted me to come and get the Koel.

Asian Koels belong to a family of birds known as parasitical cuckoos as they do not build nests of their own, but instead, lay their eggs in the nests of other birds, thereby palming off their parental duties to another.

The two common parasitical cuckoos found in the Kabini area are the Common hawk-cuckoo, also known as the Brainfever Bird due to its distinct call, and the Asian Koel.

The Common hawk-cuckoo prefers to use *Turdoides* babbler's nest, while the Koel usually uses the crow's nest. The eggs of parasitical cuckoos bear a striking resemblance to the eggs of their hosts or foster parents. This is so that the foster parents do not reject a strange egg or one that looks a little different.

Once the chick has grown and the foster parents realise that the chick isn't theirs, they see red and do their best to kill it. This was the case with the chick that had taken refuge at my house.

My colleague Nawaraj and I rushed over and managed to get hold of the chick. She was safe with us for now, but we had to make sure that we released her in a safe place. This was easier said than done, as getting rid of the crows was proving to be difficult. They followed us continuously, determined to finish off their task. I soon realised that the only hope was to release the Koel into a thick bush where the crows could not get at her.

When the Koel was released in a suitable bush, we hung around to make sure that she remained safe. After a while, the crows realised they could not get at her and slowly left the place. Crows are very intelligent birds and fascinating to watch, and there was a good chance that they may return after we leave. We had released the Koel far away from the nest where she had been born, hoping that it would make a difference. Looking at the crow's reaction, I felt that the worst might just be over. However, one can never tell.

BODY LANGUAGE

It is a commonly held belief among many people that animals have no expressions — that they are expressionless. Anybody who has had pets knows that this is certainly not the case. On the contrary, animals can be very expressive and body language plays an important role in communication between animals.

In fact body language is the primary means of conveying social information among mammals and other animal species. Some expressions can be accurately interpreted even between members of different species, with anger and extreme contentment being classic examples. Others, however, are difficult to comprehend, even in familiar individuals.

Expressions rely upon minuscule differences in the proportion and relative position of facial features, and reading them requires considerable familiarity and sensitivity towards them. They say animals have rudimentary taste buds. One thing that I know for sure is that all my dogs (seven in all, considering the years that have passed by) have had the taste buds of a gourmet chef.

One day, on a safari, I witnessed a scene that will remain etched in my memory forever. Not because anything dramatic happened but because of the expressions on the face of a wild boar that suddenly and quite unexpectedly came face to face with a spotted deer.

I was so excited that I leaned out of the Jeep to freeze the moment on film. The wild boar then turned to look at me, and with what an expression on his face at that. I am sure he was equally amused at my expression.

This is among the best wildlife moments of my life. And definitely counts among the top.

THE KURUBA VILLAGE

Close to the resort, there is a little gem tucked away and hidden from prying eyes. This is Sannemadanahalli, a small tribal village where time seems to stand still. It is a delightful little place where one can still find traditional huts of the Kuruba, the native tribes of Kabini.

The village is a charming place where one can unwind while enjoying the simple hospitality of the people. They are fiercely proud of their heritage and more than willing to share it with you.

I have spent many mornings listening to tales from the Hejman or village elder, which transported me back in time. Apart from the stories and the culture that one soaks in, you can also close your eyes and just listen to the sounds as they go about their daily lives. The sound of people working in the fields, a cow or calf mooing for attention, the crank of the handle from the little forge or just the sound of the wind rustling through the undergrowth is indeed enchanting.

No spa or meditation centre can beat this soothing experience and a visit to this village is definitely one of the highlights of a trip to Kabini.

I like to refer to the dry season in Kabini as the season of the 'Reds' as there are two species of trees, one of whose flowers are red and the other whose fruit is red, that stand out during this time. They are the Flame of the Forest and the Ficus.

The Flame of the Forest in bloom is a sight that has never ceased to hold me riveted. It is a species of tree that flowers during the dry season when the entire forest is parched. Its lovely red flame-shaped blossoms give it the common name — Flame of the Forest.

At this time of the year, when the forest is drying out, these blossoms provide life-giving nectar to the birds and bees. This is a godsend for the avid birdwatcher, as a few hours spent near one such tree can yield some excellent sightings of birds — no need to move long distances. Be still, and the birds will come to you.

Here are some interesting facts about the Flame of the Forest tree. It is sacred to the moon and is said to have sprung from the fallen feather of a Falcon imbued with Soma, the beverage of the gods. Its flowers are supposed to contain the divine drink that is offered to the deities.

During the spring festival, a temporary yellow dye is made from them. The dry twigs of the tree are used to feed the sacred fire during poojas, and its wood is used to make sacred utensils. The leaf of this tree is trifoliate — the middle represents Vishnu, the left Brahma and the right, Shiva.

The other red that surfaces around this time is the Ficus tree, the fruit of which is red in colour. The fruit not only attracts many animals and birds, but the thick canopy of these trees provides much-needed shade in the hot months when practically every other tree is leafless. The temperature under the tree is at least four to five degrees lower.

After the spectacular display of reds by the Flame of the Forest and Ficus trees, it's the turn of the Golden Shower Tree to display its spectacular yellow blossoms. The Golden Shower Tree is a native species that is present in large numbers in Kabini.

Its flowering is spectacular, with bright yellow flowers adorning the entire tree, adding much-needed colour to the forest. Also known as the Indian Laburnum or the Amaltas, this tree has multiple uses. Its bark is used as a tan and yields a red dye. Its sweetish fruit pulp is an effective purgative, even safe for pregnant women. A paste made from its roots is used to cure skin diseases and leprosy, and its leaves are reputed to heal ulcers.

The fruit is a long cylindrical pipe, and the seeds inside it are stored in little compartments encased in a strong-scented, sweetish pulp. Ripe pods are black in colour and fall whole to the ground. They do not split open to release their seeds for germination.

Interestingly, these seeds are released by animals that eat the fruit pulp. In Kabini these include bears, wild boars, and monkeys. To reach the pulp, they crack open the pods, and the seeds pass through their digestive tracts, which helps in germination and spread.

Not surprisingly, Kabini has a dream team, and the best place to watch them is when the Nelli or Amla tree is in fruit. The members of this 'Dream Team' are langur and spotted deer. When you spot a herd of spotted deer feeding, chances are that there will also be a troop of langur feeding on the trees above them.

A fruiting Nelli tree will always have a few langur on it as the fruit is much favoured by them. These are messy eaters, and as they feed, they drop a lot of fruit on the ground. The fallen fruit attracts spotted deer, providing them with a delicacy usually out of their reach. Under every Nelli tree with langur on it, one will find spotted deer enjoying a meal that they cannot get to eat on their own.

There is another interesting dimension to this relationship. They team up to warn each other of approaching predators. The langur is a primate and therefore possesses colour vision as they need to know when fruits are ripe enough to be eaten. Spotted deer, on the other hand, lack this capacity and thus poorly discriminate between motionless forms.

Langur make up for this flaw, and due to their high perch up in the trees, they can also detect predators earlier than the deer and warn about them. Deer, on the other hand, have a very well-developed sense of smell and hearing, and they reciprocate by warning the langur when they detect predators.

Together, they make a formidable team and it is not surprising that a tiger is successful only once in ten attempts in making a kill.

CULTIVATING THE WILD

Coming from a planting background, one of the many joys in my life is bringing degraded areas back to their former glory. It is a slow process, but the joy and pleasure it brings is certainly worth the long wait. I got one such opportunity when I was in Kabini.

The resort's site was once an agricultural field. The biggest disadvantage of agricultural land is the absence of trees. Crops do not grow well under trees and, therefore, they are absent in agricultural fields. Thus planting trees was the first thing we did. But trees take time to grow and to make up for this, we decided to also plant some shrubs. Only local shrubs were planted and were taken from wherever they were found: the roadside, ditches, abandoned or fallow land, and so on.

Then came the question of grass. At first, exotic lawn grass was considered as an option as this was, after all, a high-end resort. After much careful thought and much deliberation, it was decided that we should let natural grass take over. The secret to success is to do as little as possible and leave the majority of the work to Mother Nature.

The other issue was mowing the grass. We decided not to cut the grass where we had planted shrubs, the idea being to create islands of wilderness between the cottages. We decided on a balance between the wild and the cultivated, with the scales slightly skewed in favour of the wild.

It took two years for the desired effect, but the bird life on the property is now thriving.

SNAKE RESCUE

Now that the Resort is relatively wooded, thanks to our (Naturalist Department's) insisting that we abandon the cultivated look and let nature take its course, the number of snakes on the property seems to have increased or at least they have become more visible.

As you can guess, this new and, from our point of view, welcome development did not go down too well with our professional city-bred hotel management colleagues. Their idea of "hygiene" would make an ICU in a hospital proud. The usual standard phrases (another hotel management obsession—standard phrases), "the guests will get scared," "the guests will object" and so forth, were bandied about.

Rest assured no guest sees a snake; I mean, they can barely see beyond their noses. The people who see snakes are the gardeners and housekeeping staff. Luckily, they happen to be mostly local people from the surrounding villages and we therefore decided to ignore the Hotel Management Gurus and deal with the people who first spot the snake.

We told them to report to us directly whenever they saw a snake and not to harm it. I am being a little polite here; we actually threatened them with death if they harmed the snake. Surprisingly, this went down very well with them, as they already think we, especially me, are not quite normal. I mean, who tells a gardener that his job is not to mow the grass or remove weeds but to do nothing except watch nature take its course?

In rural India, yelling at people when they are caught wasting time at work is expected. I was the first person to yell at them when they did their job and appreciate them when they did nothing. It took a little getting used to, but our rural folk are not dumb; they catch on fast.

The result was that they were convinced that I was not quite there. So, nothing I do or say surprises them anymore. They put it down to my unbalanced mental state and go along with it – who wants to be troubled and yelled at by a madman who also happens, by a cruel twist of fate, to be your boss? It's easier to play along and get on with life.

Anyway, we decided that once a snake was seen, it would be in its best interest to catch it and then release it outside the compound. To accomplish this, we formed a snake rescue team within the department. We got some snake-catching gear made, and we have been quite busy since then.

THE WONDER YEARS

There is a garden in every childhood, an enchanted place where colours are brighter, the air softer, and the morning more fragrant than ever. Unfortunately, time is an ever-flowing river, like the Kabini. And before you know it, the kids have grown up and are ready to leave the nest.

I saw this young Long-tailed shrike the other day, and it felt as if only yesterday I watched its parents build their nest. It made me take a good, long look at my daughter. And I suddenly realised that she, too, had grown. That's life, I guess.

I am sure the parents of the Long-tailed shrike were used to the classic line — once the kids have left the nest, we might sell this house and move to someplace smaller.

Perhaps one of the toughest challenges of being a parent is letting go. Liberating those we've created, raised, cared for, and built our worlds around is never easy.

However, whenever I see how this unfolds in the wild, I am struck by the sheer effort the parent birds put in to ensure that their kids get the best chance to survive — and then repeat the whole thing the very next year.

We humans have it easy; another lesson we can learn from the wild.

LESSER KNOWN STAR

When we think of the 'Giants of Kabini', our minds naturally turn to elephants. Yet, there is a lesser-known giant that roams the forests of Kabini – the Gaur, also known as the Indian Bison. The gaur in Kabini holds a unique charm, distinct from its counterparts in other wildlife parks.

The gaur is a rather shy animal, making it quite difficult to observe its behaviour over long periods of time. However, for reasons delightful but unknown, they seem to have shed this shy behaviour in Kabini. This unique change in behaviour makes Kabini one of the rare places where one can observe this magnificent animal for long periods of time and very often at close quarters, creating a truly magical wildlife experience.

There is another unique feature of the gaur of Kabini. For some reason, they achieve their most magnificent physical form in this region. This makes Kabini doubly important — as one can experience the gaur in all its splendour at close quarters and for a reasonable amount of time. Sighting and observing their behaviour is a true Kabini experience often overlooked due to a genuine lack of knowledge.

One such is the lateral display, which is a behavioural pattern used by gaur bulls to establish dominance. When two bulls meet, they proceed to present their profiles by standing parallel to each other with their heads lowered and their backs hunched. Often, one of the bulls will start to circle, moving very slowly and stiff-legged, while the other stands still but shifts position to keep his broadside towards the other. This 'display' carries on till either of them accepts the subordinate position. At times, when neither bull accepts subordination, a duel occurs with the locking of horns. Such duels rarely end in death.

Another interesting feature can be observed during the rut or mating season. The onset of the rut results in extensive calling and roaming, with bulls raising their muzzles and making their characteristic rutting calls with a slightly open mouth. Most of the calling is done during dawn and dusk. There is no pleasanter sound in the forests of Kabini than that of a gaur calling during the rut.

Oh, and a bull gaur in his prime is a majestic and awe-inspiring sight.

THE TWILIGHT CHASE

Last evening's Jeep safari was full of incidents. The weather was pleasant, and the lighting was perfect for enjoying nature at its best.

The safari began with the sighting of a pack of twelve wild dogs, including pups. After watching them (for about half an hour near Sunkadakatte) we proceeded towards Tiger Tank. We waited there for a while and then decided to move on as it was getting late. We took the road going straight out via the S Bend. Close to the KV Junction, we stopped to look at a herd of gaur, one of the animals that I enjoy spending time with.

After a while, langur alarm calls rang out, alerting a herd of chital grazing nearby, to which they quickly responded with their own calls. The deer were grazing on our left, while the gaur and the langur were on our right. Something was indeed up, and the tension in the air was palpable.

What followed next was one of the most stirring sights I have ever witnessed. One of the chital persistently kept looking at a female gaur that was grazing a little ahead of the others. After a while, this female gaur started moving further away from us, along the undergrowth, snorting as she went. Suddenly, she picked up speed and flushed out a leopard from the thick bushes.

The leopard darted across the road in front of our Jeep, relentlessly pursued by the gaur, before disappearing into the undergrowth. We just stood there stunned. I have never seen anything like it before.

Taking photographs was the last thing on my mind.

SIGNS AND OMENS

Why is it that people who live close to nature are superstitious? Most people these days look down on superstition as if it was an affliction of a diseased mind. I often find myself in disagreement with them as I have my fair share of 'good signs' and 'bad omens'. One of my early heroes, Jim Corbett, was a bundle of contradictions; he always stated that he was not superstitious and that there was a rational explanation for everything. It was this outlook that enabled him to confirm that the cry of the 'Banshee' or 'Churail' was the call of a bird he had not seen before — his description of which fits well with the changeable hawk eagle or the mountain hawk eagle, whose call sounds quite like a scream.

It must be mentioned here that Corbett was of Irish descent, and as we know, the Irish are quite superstitious. I guess that could be one explanation as to why he considered killing a snake as he was setting out to hunt man-eaters a sign of good luck. In fact, he quite often ascribes his bad luck to not having killed a snake before setting out or during the course of the hunt.

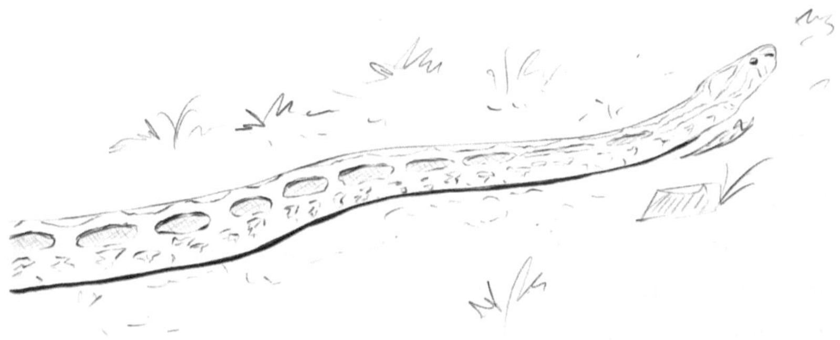

I, on the other hand, consider a snake sighting as a good sign and I was therefore quite thrilled at spotting a Russell's Viper crossing the road as I started the safari one evening. Another of my good signs is spotting a mongoose at the start of a safari. Soon up ahead, we sighted two tuskers I had named Big Boy and Little Boy. Big Boy suddenly turned and ran behind some bamboo. That surprised me, as he is quite comfortable with Jeeps around. A while later, I saw Little Boy emerge from the left and cross the road. Immediately, Big Boy came out, and both of them started pushing each other around.

It was quite obvious that Little Boy was getting the worst of the exchange so what he did next was really extraordinary. He first came up behind Big Boy and prodded him in the rear with his tusk. He then chewed on his tail! After that, he caressed him lovingly as if to make up. I have never witnessed such bonding between two tuskers. I guess boys will be boys, and will always find time to indulge in juvenile fun and games.

Hoping that my luck would hold I decided to follow the Balle River towards Bisalwadi. It is not a much-frequented route as the sightings are not great here. But it's a preferred route of mine as I enjoy the solitude of the forest as much as the animals that inhabit it. By the time I exited the park, I got to see some sambar and a pack of wild dogs, my favourite predator. There is something about the dog family that gets to me. Cats, though spectacular, somehow fail to hit the spot. I guess I am a little different from the average wildlife lover.

The signs had proved right again and I guess somebody's bad omen can be another's good luck charm indeed.

Coming back to spirits, I guess all of us who spend our lives in and around wilderness areas and jungles of the world have our pet omens, both good and bad. I guess it has to do with the fact that we realise that one can never take the wild for granted, no matter how familiar we may get with a certain patch of the jungle. Hence we start becoming aware, much like a card player or gambler, of certain patterns, a gut feeling, or maybe a heightened sense of sensitivity to our surroundings that we develop. Somehow, there are certain things that happen at certain times that warn us of good or bad things ahead. Don't ask me to explain it but there it is. This is something that the weekend 'wild lifer' will never understand or develop. This is what sets us apart from the rest; professional versus amateur or rather player versus spectator.

So do you consider me a superstitious fool? Frankly, I don't care, but in the future, be aware that the term 'sixth sense' does exist for a reason, and in the fullness of time; I suppose science will prove it right. I have always maintained that science often follows the trail blazed by superstition and not the other way around.

WELCOME RESPITES

The first rains of the season are much looked forward to by people living in the countryside. The smell of rain on dry ground is probably the most refreshing and invigorating smell on earth. I have often wondered why perfumers don't bottle it!

Rains provide a welcome respite after a dry spell, and they are one of my favourite times to go on a safari. Allow me to describe for you one such episode. We had a couple of good showers in Kabini which besides providing a welcome respite from the heat, also doused all the fires that were raging in Nagarhole and Bandipur. Actually the days are still warm bordering on hot and the rain comes down in the evenings. At least that is what happened yesterday.

The plan was to wait it out at Tiger Tank, unfortunately, the rain came down when we were there so we decided to move on. En route, we saw a few birds not always seen on an average day. The list included the Lesser yellownape, Blue-bearded bee-eater, Black-hooded oriole, Large woodshrike and the Asian paradise flycatcher. I even managed to get a decent photograph of a White bellied woodpecker.

After the rains hit, I decided to visit the Bisalwadi Kere as it had been a while since I had been there. At the KV Junction, we came across a Makhana (tuskless male elephant). At first, he seemed a bit put off by our presence so we did not approach him closely and let him have some space. Every animal has its comfort zone and it is always better not to intrude for if not disturbed, they ignore you and allow you to take some good photographs. Fortunately for us, he calmed down after a while and started nibbling on the fallen tree barks. Once he finished he came onto the road and approached us. He still did not seem too comfortable with our presence and therefore I decided to drive away.

After visiting the waterhole (which is now up to the brim, thanks to the rain), I followed the Balle River (a rain-fed stream that joins the Kabini). There is a check dam on this river, and a few puddles of water were visible in depressions in the stream bed, but otherwise, the Balle was dry. We encountered an alert group of sambar along the road, whose alarm calls we had heard before we spotted them. This enabled us to approach them carefully, and they let us come quite close, which was a pleasant surprise. They are usually quite difficult to approach. This is probably the closest I have managed to get to the sambar.

Unfortunately I did not get to see what had alarmed them. Whatever it was, had melted away.

On the way out, we saw this stripe-necked mongoose mother and child busy digging up the ground (softened by the rain) looking for goodies. This reminded me that my daughter Tara would be back for her holidays soon, and I had better stock up on some goodies for her.

All in all, it was a very pleasant evening, the rain providing a welcome respite from the heat to both me and the wildlife. Each of us went about our daily lives, neither of us encroaching on the other's privacy and at the same time, enjoying each other's company (I sincerely hope they enjoy my company as much as I do theirs).

Having lived in Kabini for so long, I'm quite used to people asking me to narrate my most memorable or thrilling experience of it. I'm sure they're quite disappointed when I sort of fumble around and am unable to pinpoint any one incident. However, I always tell them that to me the true spirit of Kabini is its elephants, and if you press me further, then they're the magnificent tuskers, Kabini's Gentle Giants.

I find them fascinating, huge . . . the largest of our land mammals, but at the same time, so calm and collected, they have an air of quiet dignity about them. And of course, the best time to view and photograph them is at the backwaters during the summer.

The Gentle Gaint

It was during an evening boat safari a couple of years ago that I chanced upon one individual and the entire experience that evening was a fine example of what to me is the true Spirit of Kabini.

He was busy grazing on the succulent reeds at the edge of the water, in a calm and happy mood. One could see that he was at peace with the world. The light was perfect for photography, but he condescended to allow us to approach him closely.

I felt that I had entered his world as we drifted close by, as he continued to feed unconcerned by our presence. I photographed him to preserve a memory. After a long while, we went our separate ways. To me that was a great experience. I had been granted entry into the world by a Giant, who, if he had wanted, could have sent me into the next world. Instead, he chose to share his world with me.

The Flute Player

I love elephants. I'm clear about that. They have given me many memorable moments in life. Some, strangely, have been bordering on the comic. I can still vividly remember this one female whom I named the Flute Player.

Interestingly, elephants feed on bark, and they love it. Bark is a food source for elephants and a very valuable one during a drought. All of them indulge in this 'delicacy' from adults to calves, as evident through this photograph.

Watching them go about debarking a tree is fascinating. Tuskers use their tusks to prise out the bark and then pull out large strips with the help of their trunk. Females are at a minor disadvantage. However, this is very slight. A fact not known to many of us is that some females have very small tusks that are barely visible under their trunks. These help them debark trees. They also take advantage of any fallen tree.

The Flute Player was a female who was 'working' on a fallen branch. She held a fallen branch in her mouth with her trunk and was gnawing the bark off, while slowly twisting the branch. She struck a pose that earned her this sobriquet. It was a truly hilarious sight.

Elephant Romance

The essence of a safari for me is not how many species you get to sight, but what you get to see them engaged in. Animal behaviour is extremely interesting, and to be able to observe it requires immense patience and a fair bit of luck.

Driving around trying to cover as much area as possible is not the best way to go about it. It pays to spend quality time with these wonderful pachyderms. My patience paid off one evening, and I got to observe what I can only call — Elephant Romance.

I was fortunate to witness a cow elephant flirting (can't think of a better word) with a bull in musth. She was practically "petting" him. He seemed interested and was checking to see if she was in estrous. However, after a while, he seemed to lose interest. The cow too, decided to call it quits and walked off after some time. The bull took off in the direction of a herd spotted in the distance and began feeding close to it. I have never seen elephants' mate, but I think I came pretty close to it that time.

Unfortunately, the flirtation remained just that — a flirtation, and did not result in anything serious.

Friends

The Kabini backwaters are an amphitheater of life. During the years that I spent in Kabini, I have been witness to many moments, dramatic and emotional, to both death and life.

In nature, everything has meaning, even death; for one's death ensures the survival of another.

One of my most memorable moments was the meeting of two giants during the drought of 2002-03. The entire forest had dried out although it was only January. Strangely, even the backwaters, usually full of lush grass, were dry due to the sun. The river had shrunk to a fraction of its size.

One large tusker was grazing, trying to squeeze some nutrition out of the dry grass. I was watching him, my mind wandering. Suddenly, out of the corner of my eye, I saw another large tusker emerge from the bamboo thicket on my right.

He walked straight up to the grazing tusker with purposeful strides. The two met and then embraced. There is no other way to describe what happened. They then continued to embrace and caress each other gently. It was poignant to watch them lean and push against each other. Not once did I see or sense any aggression between them. It was a meeting of two old friends after a long gap.

After a while, they parted and went in opposite directions to continue with their feeding. It was, and is one of my most cherished wildlife experiences.

Territorial Tusker

Last evening, we decided to go on a boat safari. The weather was favourable and we were sure of spotting some animals in the forest. Sure enough, without much delay, we spotted a tusker strolling along the banks of the Kabini. He seemed to be enjoying his leisurely walk, so we decided to observe him for a while.

At first, all seemed calm while the magnificent tusker was taking a glorious stroll. But as soon as he spotted a crocodile lazing by the water's edge he headed straight for it and chased it into the water. It was a surreal scene straight out of Gajaendramoksha – do not ask me to explain it for I cannot but for those who don't believe me, my colleague Narendran was with me and I also have photographic evidence to prove it. We assumed he didn't fancy sharing his stretch of the river with the crocodile for having successfully driven him away, he resumed his mighty gait.

A little further off the banks he chanced upon a bunch of mynas on a stump. Seemingly bothered by their presence, he drove them away. I assumed he must be on the lookout for some peace and solitude.

Luckily for us, he did not seem to mind our presence and we were able to watch his gala performance with ease.

FEATHERED JEWELS OF KABINI

Most visitors to Kabini are more interested in going on safaris and who can blame them? After all, Kabini is a paradise for those who like wildlife. However this obsession with safaris has a downside too; most of them miss the wealth of nature and wildlife that can be found outside the park. Our resort campus, for example, has a lot to offer in terms of nature and wildlife if one would only take some time to look around.

A good place to start is near the infinity pool. Yes, the infinity pool! Relax and soak in the sun but don't let your mind wander — a tough task, but one with a few rewards. Soon you will realise that you are not alone, for the pool has a resident who looks on you with mixed feelings. He is the White-browed wagtail. You will find him wandering around the place furiously wagging his tail.

When you walk back to the reception area you will in all probability come across a few sparrows. Now sparrows were once common in our cities but they seem to have abandoned them lately. Do they know something we don't? If it has rained, look around for a few muddy patches, you should find a few of them indulging in a mud bath. This might strike you as a good idea, and if it does, do change direction, and head for the Vaidyasala for a relaxing treatment of your own.

These two are not the only ones; we have many interesting birds frequenting the resort. Each is a character in their own right.

Black Tie

A Black Tie event is one where you are required to wear a Dinner Jacket. In today's world, it is the most formal dress code that there is. Though this was not always the case, one hardly comes across a White Tie event these days. Now not all of us are comfortable wearing a dinner jacket. In fact these days, it seems that most people are not even comfortable in a jacket and tie, especially within the 'wildlife' community. It seems that the more disdain one has for his personal appearance, the more of a 'wildlifer' he is. However, I digress. This should not be a rant against current fashion trends.

However, in the wild, we have one couple who is always dressed in a black tie. This is the Pied Bushchat. Pied, simply put, means black and white, and the pied bushchat male is black and white in colour. Now there are a lot of others who are similarly dressed, but the pied bushchat has a special place in my life, as a couple had decided to make a home outside my office window in Kabini.

My most enjoyable moments in Kabini were spent observing this well-dressed gentleman and his equally elegant, though understated, wife go about their daily business. As I mentioned earlier, one should enjoy the entire Kabini experience, and there is no better place to do so than from within the resort campus, where you will most certainly run into this dapper couple.

The Narcissist

Continuing from where I left off, when you leave the Infinity Pool and walk towards the Reading Lounge, you will notice a small rainwater harvesting pond nearby. This is the chosen haunt of a true narcissist. He is a small guy with a weakness for bright clothes. His preference for blue is quite striking. And in my valued opinion, he has a better grasp of mixing colours than his bigger and more famous rival, the peacock. The one in question is the Common Kingfisher.

When it comes to elegance, they say that less is more, and he seems to have mastered his art. Apart from his clothes, it is his demeanour and grace that makes him stand out as a truly elegant gent.

You will find him perched on the bushes overhanging the pond, looking intently at the water like Narcissus. However, don't let that fool you. While he may look like he is admiring his reflection (I for one would not blame him for doing so), what he is actually doing is looking for his dinner because, alas, in this day and age, even a gentleman has to work. After all, it is the Kaliyug.

If you are fortunate enough to observe him diving for his dinner, you will realise that even when delivering a fatal blow, he is grace personified, a true gentleman indeed.

The Polygamist

One evening, as I was strolling on the side along the Kabini, I chanced upon a small inlet that was well-wooded with small trees and bushes with branches overhanging the water. It was here that I stumbled upon a colony of baya weavers.

The male baya weaver is a polygamist. He has a unique system of his own that involves a lot of hard work. At the beginning of the breeding season, usually with the start of the monsoons, he starts work on a wonderful retort-shaped nest. These nests are usually built on trees standing in or overhanging the waters. The building parties of the nests consist of ten to fifty birds and comprise exclusively of males.

When the nest reaches a certain stage, the females, who until now had been absent from the colony, come visiting. They hop from nest to nest subjecting each to careful scrutiny.

Once a nest is 'approved', the female moves in and accepts its builder as her husband. After adding the finishing touches to the nest together, the female proceeds to lay her eggs. At this time, the male flies off to commence another nest close by, which in turn is approved by another female. In this manner, the male finds himself the devoted husband of three to four wives and father of an equal number of families.

Some of you may be wondering why I introduce animals and birds as characters, for is that not romanticising things a bit? I mean, do I really believe what I write? Well, the answer to that is a bit complex, and unfortunately for some, (but fortunately for me), beyond the scope of this book. Therefore, let me just continue to do what I do, and I request you to kindly bear with me.

THE LARGE-HEARTED GENTLEMAN

Big cats have always fascinated us and the tiger is no exception. A majority of the people who visit Kabini wish to see a big cat, and if possible, capture it on film. A large percentage has eventually, after multiple visits, been able to achieve that goal. Most of these photographs show the tiger very clearly, however, is that how we really see them? What makes for a good tiger-photograph?

To me, a good tiger-photograph is one that takes me there. One that gives me a sense of time, where I can almost smell the ambiance, the forest, and the stillness all around. The tiger's presence should be incidental. And that is magic. Photographs like these also give you the true feeling of a chance encounter; something not planned or prepared for.

We are fascinated by the tiger because of its mystique and aura. Tigers are rarely seen, however their presence is always felt. A picture may be worth a thousand words but somehow only a few of the photographs I have taken are able to capture and express the atmosphere in a forest, when we all know that a tiger is present but yet unseen. A wordsmith, Jim Corbett comes to mind, can convey the atmosphere beautifully — the tension, the nervous expectation and an underlying fear pulsing in the moment.

Corbett describes — "The tiger is a large-hearted gentleman with boundless courage and that when he is exterminated, as exterminated he will be, unless public opinion rallies to his support — India will be the poorer by having lost the finest of her fauna."

A tiger sighting in Kabini is always the cherry on top and no matter what one says or feels about the other wildlife, a tiger sighting is the most exhilarating experience one can have here. There are many reasons for this, mostly emotional and spiritual, the rareness of the incident, its association with the divine and so on ... and with a bit of marketing thrown in, it makes for the ultimate experience.

However, a tiger sighting is not in everyone's fate, and the biggest mistake one can make is to dedicate one's safari to trying to spot a tiger. This will kill the entire safari experience for you. My advice is to enjoy the big picture, and when you have fully immersed yourself in the experience, the gods of the forests will smile upon you and bless you with the sighting of the said gentleman. After all, in this day and age, a true gentleman is hard to find, in and outside a forest.

BISALWADI MAGIC

Bisalwadi is an important and popular waterhole in Kabini. Situated at the boundary of the tourism and core areas, it attracts a lot of wildlife especially during the summer. A watchtower situated near the waterhole gives one a panoramic view and adds much to the charm of the place as it is permitted to use the watchtower during safari timings.

A lot of people are not aware of the fact that Bisalwadi is a man-made waterhole which, in its previous avatar, used to be a cattle pen. It gets its name from a temple dedicated to Bisalwadi, a tribal deity, which was located there and which has since been relocated to the Sunkadakatte FRH and elephant camp. As you look down towards the waterhole from the watchtower you will notice a steep bund reinforced with stone masonry on the far side. The masonry has, over the years, slipped in some places creating small pathways that lead up to the bund.

Large clumps of giant bamboo grow on top of this bund, providing it with a lovely backdrop (the bamboo has since flowered and died). The area directly in front of the watchtower is fairly open with a few trees and a couple of clumps of bamboo obstructing what is otherwise a clear view of the water. From the left a fireline runs down in a straight line from the core area and meets the waterhole roughly in the middle. On the other side of the waterhole, the same fireline continues and meets the safari road that runs from Bisalwadi to the Sunkadakatte elephant camp and is often used by the wildlife to access the waterhole from both sides.

It was on a hot summer afternoon when we decided to go and spend time at the waterhole. During the wet season the water stretches all the way from the base of the tower to the bund. At this point of time the water levels had retreated and there was a thin strip of land between the bund and the water. There were no guests and we (my team and I) had the Jeep to ourselves. It is impossible to spend quality time at a waterhole when one has guests and we always grabbed the opportunity to do so whenever we found one.

The previous evening I had the good fortune to sight a large male tiger lying in the water on the far side where a portion of the bund had slipped. The evening light was shining on him and he was a magnificent sight.

Taking that into consideration we drove directly to the waterhole ignoring a herd of gaur and two elephants that we encountered on the way. This was a fortunate thing for lo and behold, cooling off in the water at exactly the same spot, was the tiger. Blessing our luck and thanking our stars, we parked the vehicle on the side of the road and walked up to the watchtower. Instead of climbing up we crouched down at the base of the tower and waited for events to unfold. The watchtower has an elephant-proof trench around it and we were on the right side of it.

The tiger was on the opposite side but directly in front of us. He seemed totally oblivious to our presence but we knew better. He must have heard our Jeep but showed no interest in us. We took our time to gaze at him through our binoculars. At that particular point in time we had decided amongst ourselves that we would not carry our cameras when we ventured into the park together so we have no photographic records of what happened next.

From our right, a herd of elephants slowly made its way down the fireline towards the waterhole for a drink. There were two tuskers with them. Simultaneously from the left another tusker came down to drink. This tusker did not notice the tiger and after drinking his fill he quietly left. The herd reached the waterhole soon after the tusker left and though they did not notice the tiger, they did disturb it and it got up, climbed the bund and lay down behind a clump of bamboo. We could clearly see its hindquarters. From its position I concluded that it had gone to sleep. In fact it did not stir for the next hour.

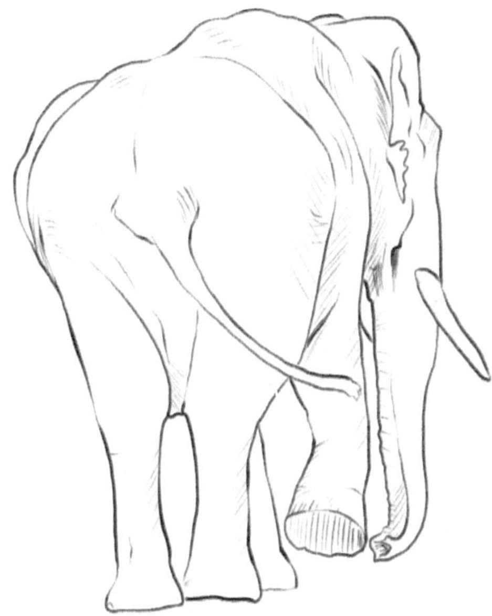

The elephant herd finished drinking and started grazing near the waterhole. After a few moments the entire herd suddenly panicked and with a lot of trumpeting and dashing around moved away quickly. They had smelled the tiger and had taken evasive action.

Meanwhile, unnoticed by us, three more tuskers were approaching the watchtower from the left. We only noticed them when we heard the cracking of bamboo. A huge tusker was feeding on a bamboo clump about forty feet from us. His two smaller companions crossed from left to right, in front of us and were soon lost to our sight. The big fellow continued to browse on the bamboo completely unaware of our presence. After a while he became alert to but not unduly disturbed, having probably smelled us soon after. He held out his ears, sniffed the air with his trunk and eventually decided that we were harmless and went back to satisfying his appetite. The silent peace between us prevailed.

A pair of sambar walked down the fireline from the left only to bolt back as soon as they reached the water's edge. All this time the tiger continued to sleep, while in the shallows, a flock of painted stork quietly fished. A most peaceful scene if there ever was one. Chances were that if you did not know the tiger's exact location you would have failed to spot him.

Time passed slowly and the temperature began to rise. It took a lot of effort on our part not to emulate the tiger and take a short nap in the shade. After what seemed an eternity, a herd of six elephants walked down from the Core area. Shortly after they started drinking they stopped and slowly left the waterhole. We thought that they had picked up the smell of the tiger and had decided to leave.

To our surprise they reappeared soon after on the far side. They then proceeded to walk, in single file, along the edge of the water right up against the bund. They were headed straight towards the tiger which had not stirred till now. The tiger still seemed to be asleep on the bund about three to four feet above and about thirty feet away from the elephants. When the elephants were about twenty feet away they climbed up the bund and started feeding on the bamboo. Two clumps away the tiger continued to sleep.

This surreal scene continued to play out for a while, the elephants peacefully grazing and the tiger fast asleep, both as, as far as we could make out, oblivious to the other's presence. We waited with bated breath for, our sleep banished for good, one of the elephants to accidentally step on the sleeping tiger. Fortunately this was not to be for suddenly one of the females sensed the tiger and charged towards the bamboo. The tiger was up and away in a flash. All this happened in the blink of an eye and we had to reassure each other that we were not hallucinating.

After a while we spotted the tiger sitting in dense cover on the bund about forty feet away from the elephants. An uneasy peace reigned, the elephants continued to feed and the tiger stayed put. Of course by now both were aware of each other's presence.

It was getting late and the time had come for us to head back. We walked back to the Jeep and as we drove away the large tusker continued to browse while his two smaller companions reappeared on the right where the first herd had been seen. They seemed the least bit perturbed with all the commotion and grazed quietly.

We left as quietly as we had come, silent spectators to an unusual afternoon at a waterhole.

EVENING AT A WATERHOLE

Water is a precious resource, and it is said that future wars will be fought over it. The same rule holds true for the wild, and there is no better place to observe animal behaviour than at a waterhole on a hot, sunny day. With this idea in mind, I decided to take the guests to a waterhole named the Tiger Tank for a lesson in jungle life.

Waiting at a waterhole is not easy for most people as it requires a lot of patience and can be pretty uncomfortable, especially if one is sitting in an open vehicle parked in the blazing sun. Add to that someone like me who is not exactly sensitive to the feelings of others, and it can become quite the ordeal.

We started our vigil in good spirits, but as it was late afternoon, there was very little activity at the waterhole. This is typical, and I was not too worried; I knew that the waterhole would soon get busy. Sure enough, after some time, I noticed that the enthusiasm among my guests was beginning to wane, resulting in some murmurings and a lot of fidgety behaviour. This was not a good sign, and I was expecting them to ask me to move to another location or drive around the park. Lucky for me, a peacock appeared and started approaching the water for a drink. I used him as an excuse to hang on for some more time.

After a while, alarm calls of spotted deer were heard in the distance, which resulted in a drastic change of mood among my guests. The calls were coming from behind the waterhole, over a bund, which put the deer out of our line of sight. Soon, langurs joined in, and I was sure that a predator was on the move, probably coming to the waterhole to quench its thirst. The calls were getting closer and increasing in intensity. We held our breath.

Suddenly, the calls stopped as abruptly as they had started. The predator had obviously changed its mind, but for what reason, I could not hazard a guess. Shortly afterwards, I noticed some movement behind the bund, and soon after, three elephants emerged with an extremely small calf — no more than ten days old, in my estimation. They were very cautious as they waited to approach the tank, protecting the calf between them. They had caught the scent of the predator and were double-checking to make sure that it was not anywhere near the water. Tigers are known to prey on elephant calves, and the family was being understandably careful.

All this while, there was a rustling to my left that was steadily getting louder. It was as if a large animal was moving through the bush. Sure enough, more elephants emerged from the bush, proceeding without hesitation towards the tank in single file.

The presence of this second family and their apparent indifference to the possible presence of a predator gave the three females the confidence to approach the waterhole. They made their way, taking care to keep the calf well hidden between them. When they reached the tank, they entered the water along with the calf. The second family drank nearby but did not enter the water. Watching elephants at a waterhole is one of my favourite pastimes, and I settled down for what I believed would be a lovely evening.

We were watching this pleasant scene for a while when a large bull gaur, appeared over the bund on the far side. A few minutes later, he was joined by two females, and together, they approached the waterhole and proceeded to drink.

After a while, the elephants left the water and, having quenched their thirst and cooled off, were in a hurry to move out. They started moving back the way they had come when, suddenly, the calf decided to suckle. This made the three females stop to let him drink. While the calf drank, the females sensed our presence, which led to a lot of rumbling and trunk-waving as they tried to get our scent. The three females bunched up to protect the calf.

After realising that we meant no harm, they calmed down and quietly melted away into the forest. The gaur finished their drink and left. The second elephant family had already moved away, leaving us in sole possession of the waterhole.

We, too, followed their lead and departed for the day. It was a lovely evening but 'uneventful' according to the guests, leaving me wondering what they expected and where they formed their opinions about the wild.

VISITORS GREAT AND SMALL

Kabini has always attracted a host of visitors, from European and Indian Royalty to the humblest of our race. However it is not only humans who find Kabini an attractive place to visit. One of the best things about living in Kabini is that you never know who will land up at your doorstep. It was an absolute pleasure to have unexpected visitors from the animal kingdom turning up at the drop of a hat.

One day I was visited by an Atlas Moth, a large winged creature usually found in the tropical and subtropical forests of Southeast Asia and Southern China. The Atlas Moth is the largest of its kind in the world, and it was seen resting on one of the resort's mud walls, to the delight of our team and guests.

The Atlas Moth can reach a mammoth size of up to 30 cm between wing tips. Due to its size, these creatures are often mistaken for small birds during flight. Its wings are beautifully decorated with different shades of tawny, maroon, white and black inside a uniquely designed boundary. Adorned with feathery antennae and a flash of colours, the moth looks all decked up to catch every single eye on its path.

The white patches seen on the wings of the Atlas Moth have a purpose apart from aesthetic beauty; they add to the insect's defences. The pattern in the shape of an eye spot is used to scare away predators.

Another interesting characteristic in most moths and the Atlas Moth is that females are larger than the males. A closer look into the world of insects, be it a moth or a beetle, never fails to surprise us.

In India Atlas Moths are cultivated for their silk in a non-commercial capacity. Unlike silk produced by the Silkworm Moth, the Atlas Moth secretes silk in broken strands. This brown, wool-like silk is thought to have greater durability and is known as fagara.

On another day, we had a visitor who had to be handled with utmost care! While we get many human visitors who need careful handling, this was a reptile — a Russell's Viper. He was found curled up in the corridor between the store and the kitchen and Siva, the Executive Chef, had passed him by without noticing. However, he was eventually discovered when he showed his displeasure on the frequent disturbances by hissing at a passerby. As mentioned earlier, when disturbed, a Russell's Viper hisses loudly, like a pressure cooker, and only bites as a last resort. He was duly rescued by our snake rescue squad which by then had been augmented with the arrival of Vineeth – a man with a passion for them. One evening, Vineeth and I, were birdwatching near the resort when, in the fading light, we spotted a bunch of large birds not far from us whose colour and shape were unfamiliar. Intrigued and excited, I stopped to look through my binoculars: seven Bar-headed Geese standing just a few yards away. This was the first time I had seen them in my life. I never expected to see them here in Kabini.

Bar-headed Geese are migratory waterfowl that come during the winter to India. They fly across the high Himalayas to reach us. They have been recorded close to Mysore and in the Nugu backwaters, which are about ten to fifteen kilometres as the crow flies from Kabini. However, I have never seen them in Kabini itself. Later, I was able to confirm that this was the first record of them here.

Mud and rain can sometimes work to your advantage. The advantage of wet mud from a Naturalist's point of view is that it is like the morning newspaper; all the events of the previous day can be read in it if you just take the trouble to look at it carefully.

I knew there was a leopard frequenting the village areas near the resort, as I had seen one some time ago. The leopard was very cautious and took great pains not to be seen by restricting its activities to the night.

I suspected that it preferred to lie up in a secure spot during the day, and the bamboo grove near the village seemed to be the best place. A few months ago, I saw fresh tracks and followed them to the bamboo grove, where I found the remains of a dog.

One morning, as I was on my way to work, I happened to glance at the mud and was pleasantly surprised. There in the fresh mud were the pug marks of the leopard. This reconfirmed not only that the leopard was still around but was thriving as well.

It's not often that one is blessed with such a considerate neighbour who not only keeps his distance and takes care not to be a nuisance but also does his civic duty by keeping the stray dog population in check.

Have you ever been swamped by frogs? I mean, literally swamped by them in the thousands? Sounds creepy, huh? Well, it's an annual affair in Kabini.

I'm talking about the Bi-coloured frogs that breed during the rains in June-July when large numbers gather around small tanks or slow-flowing streams.

The tadpoles are distinct in that they move about like shoals of fish, shifting habitats from their place of birth until they metamorphose. Large shoals of tadpoles swimming close to the surface are a common sight in the Kabini River during that period. They then metamorphose into frogs, and large numbers can be spotted all over the riverbank.

The baby frogs that emerge are rather large indeed. These 'babies' are sensitive to the sun and spend the day in the shade. As the days go by, they get more tolerant of the sun and start migrating in large groups farther into the forest, moving far from their nurseries. This is when they overrun the resort. They need to move fast because if they don't find shade, they die of dehydration — literally dry up.

The frogs are 'citizens' of the forest floor and only return to the water for breeding. During the breeding season, they move long distances to find a suitable habitat to breed.

One fine day, we had a hard-shelled visitor and a juvenile at that. I spotted this little guy across the courtyard as I was chatting up one of the Hospitality girls. I added to my eccentric reputation by jumping up mid-sentence and rushing to my office to fetch a camera. I'm sure she was not too flattered by my reaction; we're talking of an Indian Pond Terrapin.

A terrapin shell has two parts — the carapace above and the plastron below. The body within the shell is rigid, with the ribs fused to bony plates. However the parts outside the shell, namely the neck, limbs and tail, are free-moving.

I subjected the creature to a thorough 'photography session' which was desirable from my point of view, but definitely not in the best of taste. From the terrapin's perspective, it must have been a particularly humiliating and traumatic experience.

Following the 'session,' I made sure the terrapin was released in a safe spot away from prying eyes.

During my time at Kabini, I witnessed many remarkable moments in the wild. None of them were out of the ordinary — in the sense that while they were remarkable to me, they were part of the daily routine in the wild.

One evening, while I was lounging around on my veranda I heard a bird's call in the vicinity. I was in a very laid-back frame of mind and continued to relax and take it easy. I heard the bird fly away and then return after some time. I could make out that it was busy feeding off a creeper that was flowering. After a while, as I got up to go indoors, I got a brief glimpse of the bird. Imagine my surprise when I realised that it was an albino sunbird.

Albinism is a condition in birds in which some or all of the normal pigmentation is missing. It is most often inherited but can also be caused by other factors. As it is a recessive characteristic, it only shows up when a bird inherits the albino gene from both parents.

There are varying degrees of albinism, ranging from all white to just a few white feathers on an otherwise normal-hued bird. However albinism in birds is rare, occurring to any extent in perhaps one in 1800 birds.

A completely albino bird is rare, lacking any pigment in its skin, eyes and feathers. In this case the eyes are pink or red because blood shows through in the absence of pigment in the irises. The beak, legs, and feet are very pale or white. Completely albino adults are rarely spotted in the wild.

True albinos are normally less robust in other ways and often have deficient eyesight and hearing. They rarely survive long and, therefore, are barely sighted.

Partial albinism is caused by the failure of pigmentation to reach certain feathers. While this is often hereditary, other factors such as an unbalanced diet, old age, injury, or even disease and shock can cause albinism. In cases where it is hereditary, the white pattern is consistent from one moult to another. But albinism caused by environmental factors is often reversible.

I was lucky (if you can call it that) both to see as well as photograph an albino Purple-rumped sunbird. This individual was seen in the same area for a period of a month. After that, it was never seen again. I have not seen another Albino since.

I even had a visit from a rhino in Kabini, and before you get too excited, allow me to clarify: I'm talking about the rhinoceros beetle. He is the weightlifting champion of the insect world.

It can lift 850 times its body weight, making it one of the strongest living things in the world. To put this into perspective, if a human of average height and weight had the strength of the rhinoceros beetle, he would likely be able to lift an object weighing 65 tonnes.

BIRDWATCHERS

Birding or birdwatching is one of the greatest pastimes in Kabini, and with the region being home to over three hundred species of birds, this comes as no surprise. Equally entertaining or in fact in many cases rivaling this activity, is watching the birdwatchers in action!

There are many types of birdwatchers around the world, but the two most common are birdwatchers and birders. Realistically speaking, the two terms are interchangeable and can be used for anyone who observes and studies birds, no matter what their experience level or passion quotient may be. Dedicated bird lovers, however, often have strong opinions about how they refer to themselves. In general, a birdwatcher, or someone who enjoys bird watching, treats the hobby with more casualness. While they may enjoy many birds no matter where they are, they are less likely to plan explicit hikes or extensive travel only to see birds.

A birder is a more intense hobbyist. Birders frequently spend more money and are more avid about seeking out new birds. They may travel great distances to see a vagrant bird or attend a birding festival, and they may be more actively involved in the local bird community by leading bird walks, organising lectures, promoting conservation or encouraging bird-related events.

So, are you a birdwatcher or birder? Here is a rough guide. Birdwatchers own one or two field guides and won't replace them until they fall apart, use less expensive binoculars, may keep a simple list and avoid multiple records, and enjoy any birds they see on vacation, but don't specifically travel just to see birds, try to identify birds but aren't upset if they are mistaken; they enjoy the birds anyway.

Birders on the other hand, own several field guides and other bird reference books, break the bank on fancy optics and may have several different scopes and binoculars, keep multiple records, and may archive lists from year to year for comparison, travel extensively to see birds, take great care to accurately identify birds they see, and are disappointed when they miss a bird that others have identified.

So the next time you go for a bird walk in Kabini, keep an eye on your fellow guests and try to spot the difference!

Carrying on from where I left off, the question arises, what kind of birder are you? Apart from the two mentioned above, here are a few more examples ...

Twitcher: So named after the 'twitching' action they make (brought about by excitement) when they finally spot the bird they have travelled a long distance to see. A twitcher's favourite bird is the newest one they've seen. These passionate birders actively seek to add more birds to their life list, and they travel extensively to see rare or unusual birds when reported.

Citizen Scientist: he is a serious birder, often active in multiple bird conservation and education events. These birders participate in annual counts and report their findings to the appropriate organisations, and they also seek to promote the conservation of bird species and their essential habitats.

Ornithologist: he is a professional birder with advanced scientific training about not only the species but also behavior, anatomy, physiology, and bird species history. Being an ornithologist requires years of higher education, and many ornithologists lead extensive research projects to promote bird conservation. Many ornithologists specialise in very rare or endangered bird species rather than focusing on more common birds.

And here are the laws of Birding…

- The First Law of Birding: the greater the time spent searching for a rarity, the greater the chances it will be sitting on your car when you return to the parking lot.
- The Second Law of Birding: There are two sides of a tree; the side facing you and the side where the bird is.
- The Third Law of Birding: When you finally see the bird that you have always wanted to see, it will be in the last spot you thought of looking at.
- The Fourth Law of Birding: The best bird seen during a trip is usually seen in bad light, isn't calling or singing, is seen for less than a second, and is the last "trip bird".
- For a birder, a bird in a bush is worth two in the hand.

THE VIP VISIT

The Sunkadakatte Elephant Camp located in the heart of the Tourism Zone in Kabini is a lovely place to visit. Domesticated elephants of the Forest Department along with their handlers are stabled here. The elephants have a relaxed and sedate life; apart from providing joy rides to tourists in the morning, there is precious little to do.

During the annual Dasara procession in Mysore a select few are sent off to participate in it. They reach Mysore a month in advance to prepare for the ceremony which includes getting used to city traffic.

However, they are officially members of the forest department, and as is usual in India, when an important dignitary visits, they are required to put their best foot forward. I realised this one day when I happened to visit the camp and found all the elephants missing.

On inquiry, I was told that they were expecting the Chief Minister, and therefore, the elephants were being given an elaborate bath. I quickly went to their bathing spot and watched them being washed and readied for the VIP visit.

It was my most amusing experience at Kabini. I guess at the end of the day we are all subjected to India's VIP culture.

MOTHER AND CHILD

The elephant is best described as a 'family animal'. The social structure of an elephant herd or family plays a key role in the upbringing of young pachyderms. It's through this social structure that elephants grow up to develop well-rounded personalities.

The breakdown of this structure has led to much aberrant behaviour among elephants, best witnessed on a large scale in elephant calves orphaned due to poaching and culling across the African continent.

These orphaned elephants were relocated to other areas. During adolescence, these elephants were spotted displaying aggressive behaviour towards rhinos, causing a number of rhino deaths. To control them, an adult male elephant was introduced to the area, and this behaviour underwent a dramatic transformation, with the orphans no longer showing aggression. Clearly, they needed proper guidance from an adult male.

The significance of family bonds is best witnessed in the relationship shared between an elephant mother, her calf and another related adult female. While I strive not to endow animals with human sentiments, I find myself 'struggling' when I witness such behaviour.

The sheer sense of amusement and tenderness in these interactions is undoubtedly staggering. Words cannot adequately express it; sometimes, I wish humans behaved more like elephants.

They say that a son is a son until he gets married, but daughters are forever. Poor married male souls like us have realised the truth in that statement over the course of our marriages. However, if you feel that you have it bad, wait until you come face to face with an elephant mother and her female calf.

Now, in your most private thoughts, you may see more than a passing resemblance between an elephant mother and your mother-in-law. You should thank your stars that the resemblance is purely cosmetic.

An elephant mother and her female calf arguably share the closest bond in the animal kingdom. For starters, the gestation period of an elephant is close to two years, and as we share almost the same life expectancy, this is indeed a big deal. A female elephant will remain with her mother till her mother's death. She will learn about her life, where to go, what to eat, and how to survive from her. She will also depend on her when she herself first becomes a mother.

A lot of knowledge essential to the survival of the herd and the species is transmitted from mother to daughter. It should, therefore, come as no surprise that elephant herds are led by the matriarch, the oldest female in the herd, who is usually a grandmother. In this matrilineal structure, the mother and daughter relationship is of the utmost importance. So, the next time you see an elephant herd, thank your stars that your wife is not one.

This enduring bond between a mother and child is even more so in the case of herbivores. However, this is not to take away from predator mothers, but that is a topic for another story.

Herbivore mothers put themselves at risk during their pregnancy, as being pregnant slows down their reflexes and makes them more vulnerable to predators. After they give birth, they are even at a higher risk as they have to now look after and protect their offspring. However, nature has its own unique way of minimising the risk. Do you know that herbivores are born fully formed and can start walking almost from the time of birth? Contrast this with predator young that are born blind.

One of the most fulfilling experiences in Kabini is observing the interaction between mothers and their young. Now, most of us usually ignore a herd of deer as they are, luckily, quite plentiful in Kabini. The next time you spot a herd with young in it, I suggest you stop and watch them for a while. I would recommend the sambar for no particular reason except that they are not seen as often as the chital.

This special bond is usually not visible to the casual observer, especially in the case of the deer family, as it is quite challenging to read any emotion into their faces. However, on rare occasions, we witness this special bond manifesting itself into raw courage, and this almost always involves the prospect of death.

A few mornings ago, I was lucky enough to witness this special bond during the boat safari. The characters partaking in this unfolding drama were — a beautiful female sambar, her bewildered fawn and a pack of wild dogs.

Right from the beginning, the sheer number of wild dogs gave them a secure advantage over the sambar mother — who was fighting single-handedly. The pack had successfully pulled down the calf despite the mother's best efforts to ward them off. The climax of the event seemed pretty obvious to us onlookers, and I pondered the fate of the fawn.

But by the time I reached the spot, there was a very different scene unfolding before my eyes. The mother was in no mood to back down and surrender the carcass of the fawn to the savage pack and fought tooth and nail to keep them at bay. Now, a determined pack of dogs are formidable predators, and a female sambar is fair game. However, despite these facts, the sambar mother endured a heroic fight to the finish.

Very rarely have I witnessed such raw courage, especially in what was a lost cause — the sambar fawn was already dead, and no amount of courage was going to change that. But this incident changed my perception of the deer family, for behind those inscrutable faces lurks raw emotion like the kind you've never seen before.

As far as emotions go, it was one of the defining wildlife moments of my life.

THE STILLBORN AND THE GAME OF LIFE AND DEATH

Sometimes, death comes at the most unexpected of moments — moments that are beyond comprehension to us lesser mortals. Nature has its own rhythms and reasons, and as much as we try to attune ourselves to them, she has a habit of taking us by surprise. She reminds us that despite the knowledge and control we think we have gained over the world, in reality, we are nothing but pawns in the great game.

The beginning of a new life is always a special moment, especially for an elephant mother who has carried her child for almost two years. A new life is a new beginning, which is our ultimate purpose in life — to ensure the survival of our genes and species by bringing forth a new generation. Death is not expected to come knocking at the time of birth.

Unfortunately, one day, this happened. An elephant mother had given birth to a stillborn calf. I was on a safari and spotted the heartbroken family consisting of two adult females and three other juveniles of various ages standing beside the body.

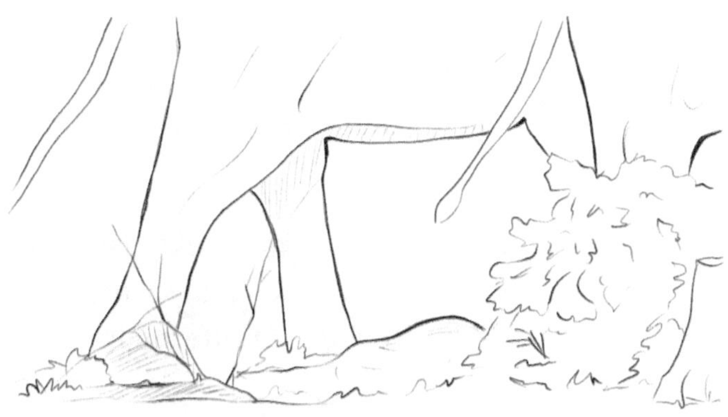

An elephant pregnancy lasts almost two years (around 22 months), and after such a long gestation, giving birth to a stillborn calf can be devastating. The family was loath to leave the body, and elephants are known to grieve the death of a family member. There have even been instances recorded of them carrying their dead calves for long periods of time. This family would remain with the body for some time.

As I stood there silently watching the scene, I heard another elephant calling from the opposite bank. I looked through my binoculars — it was a tusker in Musth.

On my right was a life snuffed out before it even began, and on my left was the foundation of a new one. The tusker was a splendid specimen in the prime of life and in full Musth, signalling to the world and female elephants in particular, that he was a prime candidate for a mate, one that would ensure that their offspring would have the best possible genes with the maximum chances of survival.

It is said that the only thing certain in life is death. It comes stealthily, creeping up on you from the day you are born. But when it comes, it can be devastating, especially for those left behind. But is death really such a bad thing? It is, after all, the circle of life, for in the wild, with death comes regeneration.

This is played out vividly and simply in the predator-prey relationship. Predators kill to live; the death of one herbivore sustains the life of a carnivore and its family. In turn, the death of plants sustains the life of herbivores, for after all, plants are living things and herbivores are plant predators. Besides this, the death of the old and weak creates space for the flourishing of the young and strong, thus ensuring the health of their species as a whole.

After that rather macabre safari, the next day's safari was a refreshing experience. Not too far from the family in mourning, another family with a newborn were enjoying the afternoon sun. Two other females were feeding on the tender reeds growing in the shallow water near the river bank.

The large tusker in musth, as seen during the previous safari, was busy on the Bandipur side. A few females loitered nearby, and he followed them into the forest. I saw one female lingering away from the rest, and he quickly caught up with her. Only in two years will we know if this flirtation will lead to the birth of another.

Another tusker was nicely framed by the giant bamboo growing near Sunset Point, which made for a lovely photograph. Life goes on, and new births will replace those that are lost. It has always been like this and will continue to be so until extinction catches up with us.

MYSTERY OF THE CORACLES OF SOUTHERN INDIA

Most people, at least those living in southern India, are familiar with the coracle and would have taken a joy ride in one while on holiday. We usually don't give much thought to its origins, assuming that it is a traditional craft that ply on the rivers of the south.

I felt the same way until sometime last year when I had a few Irish guests with me. They mentioned in passing that the coracle was very similar to the boats once found in Irish rivers. At that time, it occurred to me that the British could have introduced the design during their time in India. After a while, I filed this piece of information at the back of my mind and promptly forgot about it.

Last night, while reading a book about Scotland, I came upon the term 'coracle loads'. That prompted me to dig a little deeper, and this is what I came up with.

The history of the coracle is more about fishing than water transport, apart from a few exceptions. Before the Industrial Revolution, when rivers were not used as sewers, Britain had many salmon rivers where fishing was practised using coracles, including the Thames, which is now attracting salmon because of many years spent on a clean-up. Coracle fishing, I believe, is still practised on three rivers in Wales: the Towy, Taf, and Teifi.

The earliest record we have of coracles is from Julius Caesar, who, while fighting in Spain in 49 BC, ordered his troops to make wickerwork boats covered with hides of a type he had seen in Britain some years previously. Some historians now believe he was referring to a seagoing craft. Later, in 1188, a person named Gerald de Barry, the Bishop of Cork, while visiting Wales, described coracles but did not record precisely where he saw them.

In the year 1360 during the rule of Edward the Third, Froissart (a French author) wrote about the invasion army from England to France carrying a baggage train of more than six thousand carts in which small boats of boiled leather were crewed by three men who rowed and fished. Later in the time of Henry the Fifth, Raphael Holinshead, an English chronicler, records in his chronicle of plans for another expedition to France (invasion) in 1414 of the provision of 'boats to pass over rivers covered with leather'.

In Wales, a collection of writings (The Mabinogion) dating from before the thirteenth century references a 'leather bag' boat. In the fourteen hundreds, the Gododdin poem reads, "He would kill a fish in his coracle". Later poems in the next century recall a coracle covered in black skin from a black bullock and waterproofed with tallow cake.

It is pretty clear that coracles (from the Welsh "cwrwgl") have a history dating back thousands of years. The coracle was originally covered with animal skins, and in some countries, they are still made this way. In Wales, they are now skinned with calico, which is waterproofed using a bitumastic paint. There are still a few excellent resources for those interested in researching the subject. One, The National Coracle Centre, is to be found at Cenarth Falls, Newcastle Emlyn, Dyfed and has a display that illustrates the history and diversity of the craft. It also mentions that twelve people have licenses to fish the River Teifi for salmon and sea trout using the coracle. The Centre can supply the woven, Teifi-style coracle and instruct in its use.

Coracles have been used in the British Isles since pre-Roman times. While their prime use is transport and fishing, they have also been recorded as being used militarily and by the security forces. There is clear evidence that Arthur Wellesley, First Duke of Wellington, used them during his campaigns in India.

Coracles are found not only in the British Isles and Ireland but also in India, Vietnam, and Tibet. Until recently, they were found in Iraq, and reports, currently unverified, exist of them in Norway and close to Chernobyl.

Coracles have not been seen in Scotland for 150 years but were in use in Ireland until the late 1940s. They are, however, principally to be found nowadays in three West Walian rivers, namely The Teifi, The Towy and The Taf. Here, they are used for net fishing, with the net being held between two coracles that drift down with the current, taking a salmon or sewin at restricted times of the year. All these coracles, however, have to be licensed. While their numbers are dwindling rapidly, traditional coracle builders remain on the Severn at Iron Bridge and Shrewsbury. In its heyday, towards the end of the last century, there were more coracles to be found on the River Severn than on any other river in the British Isles.

The principal use of these coracles on the Severn at Iron Bridge was as a ferry, as there were very few bridges over that river in the area, and the locals resented having to pay a toll on the famous Iron Bridge. At Shrewsbury, they were used principally for rod and line fishing. There is also a tradition of coracles in North Wales, and they were to be seen until the 1950s in the Llangollen section of the River Dee.

Coracles are distinguished from other river craft by their weight, construction and propulsion. The coracles are traditionally made of willow or ash laths and covered with calico or canvas impregnated with pitch and tar or, more recently, bitumastic paint. They weigh between 25 and 40 pounds and so can be carried on the shoulders of the coracle man who frequently, in the case of the fisherman, would walk 5–10 miles before drifting down with the current.

They are invariably propelled with a single paddle held in two hands over the bow, executing a figure of 8 movement. Fishermen use a similar stroke but with one hand only over the side of the craft, permitting the holding of the net in the other. The Coracle Society actively seeks to preserve and protect the tradition of old coracle makers and users, of whom there are few. It also encourages a new wave of coracle makers who are increasing in numbers and are very much the product of the excellent coracle-making courses held at the Bewdley Museum, which is currently held at the Greenwood Trust in Iron-Bridge.

My personal theory is that the coracle was introduced by British troops fighting Tipu Sultan under the command of Wellington (who, being Anglo-Irish, would have been familiar with the craft). Like many other things, the coracle got so assimilated into Indian culture and way of life that its origins were lost. This would also explain why it is not found anywhere else in India.

It would be interesting for someone to dig deeper and get to the bottom of this.

CHASING THE LIGHT

Light is probably the most important factor to consider when taking a great photograph. When taking pictures, it is critical at times to be in the right place at the right time to get the perfect lighting, especially when you're dealing with the sunrise or sunset. The same applies to wildlife photography as well. Without light, photography simply does not exist.

In fact, the word photography comes from the word "photo", a Greek word meaning 'light'. Before you can understand photography, you must first understand light. Even if you have the most sophisticated camera and the most expensive and sharpest lenses, your photographs would be impossible without light, and your cameras and lenses would be useless. It is also amazing to see how quickly light can change in a matter of minutes.

The backwaters of the Kabini are extremely well suited for wildlife photography, especially during certain times of the year when the water levels recede. This makes the region more like an open plain rather than a tropical forest — which means an abundance of light.

Knowledge of the light conditions during various parts of the year is essential. For example, during winters in Kabini, there is an hour (at most) of magical light between 5 pm and 6 pm each day. An evening spent following the light rather than tracking a subject can be very rewarding. This essentially means exploring certain areas at certain times to find something to reflect the light back into your camera.

The best way to do this during the winter is to take the evening boat safari. When one begins the safari, one is driving into the evening sun, and all the sightings that occur are backlit. While this is not usually considered ideal for great photography, it does present some challenging conditions in which you can explore different techniques. If one is lucky, one gets some tall bamboo to block the backlight. It is, therefore, a better idea not to waste too much time at such places but instead head for certain spots. The secret is to get to these spots at the right time.

The Mastigudi Watchtower is one such spot. The other great place is on the Bandipur side near Kakankote, where the river takes a turn to the left. This puts the sun behind you. By the time you reach this place, the timing is usually perfect. If you cannot reach this place on time, it is better to turn the boat around and wait near Sunset Point.

On the way back, it is better to hug the Bandipur bank as this part gets the evening light for a longer period of time. But in the end, you need something to reflect that light back into your camera, and that is why I call it chasing the light. You are always running around with one eye on the light and one eye on the bank, looking for that elusive object! However, with the perfect light, almost anything will do.

The morning boat safari provides you with the best possible light conditions, as the sun is behind your back. Winter mornings can be misty, but the light turns magical once it lifts. Unfortunately, the sightings of large mammals are usually better during the evening safari.

Over the years, I have developed a soft corner for the area around the Mastigudi Watchtower. During the cold and dry seasons, this is a magical spot. However, it is quite busy, as many safari Jeeps pass through the area. Very few of them actually stop, as it is not really considered a 'hot spot'.

The Watchtower is just a landmark and is not open for tourists. It overlooks the backwaters at the confluence of the Balle and Kabini Rivers. The entire bank is lined with Giant Bamboo that grows in clumps and meets at the top, creating what I call 'Gateways' through which the wildlife must pass on their way to the river.

When the dam is full, a small inlet of water forms, much like a small cove. As the waters recede, more of the open area, along with a slight depression, is exposed. The soil in this depression remains moist, and some pools of water also stay behind. This attracts a lot of wildlife, mostly spotted deer, wild boars, gaur, and elephants.

A few crocodiles can usually be found basking on the banks. The usual waders, storks, herons, and so on are also around. I once saw a tiger there, but that is immaterial to the place's charm. If you happen to go to Kabini, insist on being taken to the Watchtower.

As mentioned earlier, at the beginning of the cold season, this place is best approached by boat (when the water level is still high enough), and the light is magical.

While everyone enjoys a visit to Kabini to witness the 'theatre' in the forest, many visitors miss the drama that unfolds in the sky. The skies above Kabini are among the most dramatic that I have ever seen. The moods are several, varied, and ever-changing. Kabini has them all, from clear blue skies to theatrical monsoon skies.

It is unfortunate that few of us have the time to observe our skies, as they can be ranked as the best of nature's creations. One moment, they are calm, and the next, threatening — looking at and observing the changing nature of skies is like looking into a crystal ball. They are the advance warning given by nature and foretell what is about to unfold in the immediate future.

Apart from this, there is the sheer beauty of a sunset or a sunrise. Cloud formations add a dramatic twist to the skies. Hence, the next time you find yourself, do take some time out and look up — you won't be disappointed. It is no wonder that people look heavenwards for inspiration and hope.

Or as the renowned wildlife photographer Hugo Van Lawick so succinctly put it, "all you need is a sunset and an animal doing something".

And then there is the monsoon season. The monsoons are magical and are the most dramatic season as far as weather goes. Photography during the monsoon is also a challenge most people prefer not to take up. To truly bring out the monsoon effect, it is best to incorporate the habitat between yourself and the subject. Unfortunately, most wildlife photographers call this clutter, as they think it clutters the image.

To truly enjoy the beauty of the monsoon and indulge in some photography at the same time, it is best to choose an overcast day with a hint of rain. It might not be considered ideal weather for photography, but it is the best the monsoon can offer — a perfect monsoon day — everything lush green, the forest in all its splendour. When the light breaks through, it can be mesmerising.

During heavy rains, play around with your shutter speed to capture drops or streaks of rain. Most importantly, animal behaviour changes in the monsoon, making for some unique moments waiting to be captured on film.

A TRUNK FULL OF TALES

Elephants are lovely creatures and fascinating to watch. What I like most about them is the fact that, on account of their elephantine memories, they literally have a trunk full of tales to narrate. Unfortunately, however, I can't speak 'Elephant'.

And I am the poorer for it, but one can only lament one's fate for so long. One needs to rise to the challenge. I did so by trying to read their body language to try and understand them. This was all very well, but I still could not communicate sufficiently to listen to their yarns.

While I could not listen to their stories, I am fortunate to have a few stories of my own that involve these gentle giants. I really enjoyed these encounters, and I am sure they did, too. I often imagine them chuckling to themselves while they recounted the same stories to their friends later.

I present below a few interesting encounters I had with these gentle giants.

Swimming elephants

They say that pigs might fly. I am not so sure about that, but I know that people are equally surprised when I tell them that Elephants swim. Yes, they do, and they are very good at it too. Surprised? Don't be. After all, they have four strong legs that act as pistons and the most valuable of all swimming tools — a snorkel.

Calves swim as well as adults, and they have no inhibitions about entering the water. One of the most unforgettable sights in Kabini is an entire herd of elephants, including mothers and babies, swimming across the river.

If the herd is spotted swimming across the river late in the evening when you happen to be in the boat, then it is even better. One, you can observe them from a close but safe distance, and two, you can photograph them as they swim across. However, you will be surprised as all one can see is a jumble of trunks and glimpses of backs.

Once across, they usually have a dust bath before disappearing into the undergrowth. Some even roll around in the mud; it is a truly surreal experience!

Naturecures

As mentioned before, one thing brightens up an otherwise ordinary safari: a sighting that highlights behavioural aspects. I was lucky to witness a tusker medicating himself one evening. Sounds surprising? Yes, it is true that wounded animals have no doctors to rush to. However, they have a wealth of knowledge on how to medicate themselves with nature's remedies.

I saw this large tusker browsing on bamboo from a distance and turned the boat toward him. He was so far away that it took us about ten minutes to reach him. He seemed content to browse, and we decided to spend some time watching him. However, he suddenly stopped beside a ditch containing muddy water and began squirting mud on himself.

This is quite typical elephant behaviour, and we were not surprised. My boatman Shivraj and I noticed that he was trying to target his rear left leg. A look through the binoculars confirmed the presence of a wound — a round hole about a few inches in diameter. To get the mud on the wound, he sat and rolled in it.

He finally got up and wandered away. He wasn't thirsty; he was merely taking his medication for the day.

David and Goliath

We have all heard of the biblical story of David and Goliath, in which a young David defeats and slays the giant Goliath in battle. The story is now synonymous with overcoming great odds with courage and conviction. In Kabini, each year, one can experience a similar battle being played out in the backwaters between a giant and his smaller adversary. The David of Kabini is the river tern and the giant? The elephant, of course.

Every year, as summer approaches, the gates of the Kabini dam are opened to let water out for irrigation downstream. When this happens, the waters recede, and small islands are formed in the backwaters. These islands, being moist, are full of fresh succulent grasses, making them a paradise for herbivores in the dry summer.

However the elephants are the only herbivores able to access them due to their excellent swimming abilities. These islands also attract river Terns, not as feeding grounds, but as breeding grounds. River terns are ground nesters, and these inaccessible islands provide a safe haven from predators. The only problem is that the elephants can inadvertently trample upon the nests. And thus, the seeds of an epic contest are sown.

River terns flock together and mob and dive-bomb the elephants in an attempt to drive them away from the islands. Watching this contest unfold is one of the wonders of the natural world. And more often than not, the river terns are successful in driving away the elephants.

SUBMERGED WORLDS

The Kabini backwaters are a breathtaking sight during the monsoons. Over 60 sq km in size and, in places, almost 4 km across, they will leave you thoroughly captivated. Unknown to many, these placid waters hide the old world, for hidden under these waters are nuggets of history that are fast disappearing from the memories of its erstwhile residents.

The Kabini unfolds its secrets hesitantly, as deep beneath these waters lies the old villages that once lined its banks but were submerged in 1974 when the Kabini dam was built downstream.

Every once in a few years, the weather gods decide to wreak their vengeance by denying us life-giving rain. Amazingly this is also when the past reappears from the depths to remind us of bygone days. One of these villages is the old Karapura Village.

It's an interesting sight as the remains of the village huts can be seen, bricks can be found strewn about, and even an old temple is visible. However, the most intriguing of all is a square formation of stones. The mind runs riot. Could this be the spot where the village elders met in the past to discuss and debate village affairs? One just needs to close their eyes to imagine them seated there. What wonderful tales they could tell us!

While the world of the ordinary man lay downstream, the waters concealed a different world upstream. The two worlds coexisted and were indeed intertwined, mutually dependent on each other for survival. But the world upstream was one of royal pomp and splendour, far removed from the humdrum lives downstream.

A royal road used to link the Princely states of Mysore and Malabar, this single-lane highway cut through the dense forests of Nagarhole — what a journey it must have been. An iron bridge, erected in 1880, spanning the Balle River still stands despite being submerged for over thirty years. Mastigudi, a famous temple dedicated to a tribal deity, was situated adjacent to this road. The weary traveller would have paused to offer his prayers to the God of these dark and deep woods — Masti Amma. Interestingly, she shares the temple with the Remover of Obstacles — Lord Ganesha. The idol, remarkably, is hewn from a single rock.

A remnant of the past, Lord Ganesha's presence strangely did not seem to have helped his brethren — the elephants. The Mastigudi temple is where prayers were offered to Lord Ganesha prior to the start of the famous *khedda* operations.

The *khedda* is a method of capturing wild elephants by driving them into a stockade with the help of domestic ones. This system was introduced into the Mysore area by GP Sanderson, a British forest officer who studied the system in Assam. As many as 36 such operations were conducted here. Interestingly the remnants of the stockade can still be seen below the waters today.

Annually, as the famous elephant congregation begins on the banks of the Kabini, Lord Ganesha rises from the depths to watch over his living manifestations as they peacefully go about their lives. The remnants of the stockade, too, rise to remind us of the sins we have committed in the name of Lord Ganesha on his ilk.

Ironically, every year, when the Mastigudi temple emerges from the depths of the Kabini, all the Naturalists and Safari drivers from the resorts in Kabini, along with members of the Forest Department, regardless of their religious affiliations, perform a special Puja to seek the blessing and protection of the Goddess Mastigudi and Lord Ganesha for an incident-free and safe safari season.

WHAT A HOOT

I have a thing for owls, and while there is no denying it, I cannot for the life of me offer any plausible explanations — I just like them. Could it be because they look so wise and only come out at night? Well, most of them, at least.

Unfortunately, owls have a terrible reputation in Indian folklore as they're considered to be the harbingers of death. The reason for this is not known. Fortunately for me, though, we had quite a few owls that could be spotted around the resort campus.

When I first moved to the resort in Kabini, there used to be a barn owl that would perch on a tree close to the swimming pool. He would be present there every night, with clockwork precision. Apart from the barn owl, there were a couple of brown fish owls that could be seen near the Reading Lounge — the resort had not yet opened fully, and I would spend the nights visiting these nocturnal pals of mine.

Once the resort opened fully, we would have to do Night Duty on rotation, and my turn would come roughly once a month. As you guessed, I would spend a good part of the night searching for owls.

One night I decided to expand my search by walking down the road that led to the village in search of owls. It was around 1 am when I started my walk, and the moon had risen, so I did not need a torch to see where I was going. Walking in the night is another one of my unusual pastimes, and I enjoy testing my ability to navigate in the dark. However, that day, thanks to the moon, the going was very easy, and I stopped to check every tree, electric post and fence post without any luck. No owls.

Deciding that a change of tactics was called for, I stopped and waited at one place and listened for calls but again had no luck. A little disheartened and irritated, I decided to try the river bank near the resort. As I passed the resort gate on my way to the river, I saw a shape fly and land on a fence post. Sure enough, it was what I was searching for: a Mottled wood owl.

The guy kept flying from perch to perch, and I had a great time stalking it in the dark. After some time, it flew into a banyan tree in the resort.

I lost sight of it in the tree and got back onto the road when another one suddenly took off from a fence post and flew towards a peepul tree beside the road. I tried my best to locate it but was unable to do so.

I stood there wondering what to do when it called. It gave a call that I had not heard before — a hoot. I got a little confused as to whether it was a Mottled wood owl or not. Suddenly, another one flew past me and onto the tree. Fortunately, I could locate it and get the beam of my torch onto it. This was definitely a Mottled wood owl. I was watching it looking back at me when it gave the typical call of its species. It kept looking at me and called repeatedly.

Quite happy with my night's work (the whole exercise lasted more than two hours), we went our separate ways. I returned to the resort, but the owl decided to stay put in the tree. On the way back, who did I bump into? It was the Mottled wood owl from the banyan.

But I was very intrigued by the call I had heard before. I was pretty sure that what I had seen was a Mottled wood owl, but I was confused about the call and needed some reconfirmation.

A few days later, I was sitting in my office when I heard an owl call. It was a softer version of the hoot I had heard the other day. I got out of the office and managed to trace the call. After a while, I was able to finally locate the owl, and I got my answer. It was my old friend, the Mottled wood owl. He gave another hoot and flew away into the darkness.

A few nights later, Bernie, my dog, woke me up at 3 am to go to the loo. Muttering, I got up and took her outside. As she was doing her job, I once again heard the hooting call coming from a tree in the distance. I was unable to see the owl, but this time, I was sure who it was — the Mottled wood owl.

Once the resort began to become popular, my friend from the swimming pool, the barn owl, became skittish and would only make the occasional appearance. The presence of too many people and the now bright pool lights had quite obviously disturbed him.

It then struck me that I should try to induce him to roost and eventually nest on the property by building a nice little home comprising a 'nest' box. There are a couple of large trees around the resort, and I felt that the large ficus near the Reading Lounge would make an excellent home for him. This ficus tree, besides being large, was also isolated. And it seemed perfect to me. Unless the owl thought like me, he would not come to reside there, whatever the charms of the tree.

'Nest' is not the appropriate word to use in connection with barn owls, as they build no nests as such, preferring instead to lay eggs on a layer of pellets accumulated at their roosting spot. Such sites are deep, spacious cavities in trees, dark corners of barns, churches, old buildings, or even gaps in straw stacks.

While owls may readily accept a nest box, they will initially use it to roost, and it can take them as long as two years before finally breeding. I tied the nest box securely to a fork in the tree. I left Kabini soon after and returned five years later to find that my carefully chosen tree had fallen during a storm, and nobody had any recollection of the home I had built for my friend.

MISTY MORNING SAFARIS

It's early morning on the Kabini, and believe me, early mornings in Kabini can sometimes put one into a philosophical frame of mind and morning safaris during the winters especially so. The silence, the mist, and the cold transport you into a zone where your imagination can run riot.

Sometimes, one can get poetic and be reminded of the works of some of the greats. While poetry is not quite my forte (or cup of tea, to be perfectly honest), the works of Robert Frost do occasionally spring to mind; after all, he did write about the woods. I quote Frost: 'The woods are lovely, dark and deep, But I have promises to keep, And miles to go before I sleep, And miles to go before I sleep.'

The primary conflict in this famous poem (which, thanks to Nehru, most Indians are familiar with), is between an attraction toward the woods and the pull of responsibility outside of the woods. What do the woods represent? Something good? Something bad? The woods are sometimes a symbol of wildness, madness, and the looming irrational.

This is the classic conflict within each of us: the conflict between what we want to do and what we have to do. Fortunately for me, there was no conflict, as exploring the Kabini woods was part of my job.

Returning to more mundane matters, misty winter mornings are my favourite time to be on a boat safari. While it might be a little low on sightings, it is unmatched in terms of the atmosphere.

You must be wondering why I am making such a statement. After all, aren't wildlife sightings what we are after when we go on a safari? Let me try to explain why sightings are not always the reason for a great safari.

A winter boat safari in Kabini is the best way to start your day. In my opinion, it's a perfect start to the day. There's usually a slight nip in the air, and with a little bit of luck, one can see the mist gently rising from the water as one makes their way towards the National Park. The visibility is low, and one proceeds slowly. There is an air of expectancy and anticipation on board — what's in store for us up ahead?

The curtain of mist slowly dissipates as the sun rises, adding a dash of mystery to the proceedings. After a period when anticipations and expectations slowly build up, paradise, as we know it, is finally revealed.

Another advantage is that one is rewarded with a spectacular sunrise. The rising sun gives the entire area a surreal look. And if you are lucky, you come across local fishermen in their coracles gathering their nets and inspecting their catch. You could even pull over alongside on your way back and pick up fresh fish for your lunch! Need I say more?

Of course, this is just the beginning. The entire park is waiting to be explored up ahead, and as we who have lived in Kabini know, she reserves her best for those who listen and adapt to her rhythms. And what better way to do so than from the water early in the morning?

A TALE OF TWO GIANTS

The backwaters of the Kabini need no introduction as it is well known among wildlife enthusiasts both in India and abroad. I have spent a decade on its banks, guiding and introducing visitors to its spectacular wildlife. During my time I was fortunate to witness many moments, a few of which I have described previously on this forum.

Those of us who live and work in the wilderness and in close contact with wildlife are often faced with dilemmas. One such is the temptation to project human characteristics and qualities onto wildlife, known as anthropomorphism and personification. This is something that many writers are guilty of and I have tried my best to avoid falling into this trap.

This is especially problematic as the attribution of negative human qualities onto animals is one of the causes for their persecution and decline. For instance the projection of the wolf as an embodiment of evil has led to their persecution and extermination in Europe. While anthropomorphism as a literary device has been widely used by many authors, one needs to be extremely sensitive to ensure that no negative associations are formed in the minds of our readers.

The far bigger dilemmas arise when it comes to injured or sick wildlife. Do we interfere or not? Do we let nature take its course? And when the individual animal is one whom we have seen and observed over long periods it only complicates matters further. There is no doubt that, in cases like this, a strong emotional bond is created between man and animal — a bond that brings with it a wide range of human emotions.

Among all my experiences in the wild there is one that stands out, one where I had to face both these dilemmas — the poignant last days of a well know tusker and the unlikely bond that developed between the tusker and an old bull gaur.

The tusker in question was a familiar figure — a gentle giant and a true gentleman that I had seen off and on for about five years. An extremely trusting individual who allowed one to get very close and blind in the left eye, he was one of the most easily recognisable tuskers in Kabini.

One day while out on safari I noticed that he had an injury on one of his legs of which I made a mental note and hoped that it would heal quickly. He did not seem to be in much pain and was going about his business as usual.

The next time I saw him, after a rather long gap, he had deteriorated noticeably and his wound was extremely grave. He was favouring his injured leg, not being able to put much weight on it. After a few days he took refuge in the river — spending most of the day submerged in water.

There is a saying among the elephant men of the North-East that when a male elephant knows that he is nearing the end of his life, he finds a river to die in. The rational explanation could be that sick and wounded elephants seek out water because due to the buoyancy factor they are able to get relief (easier to take the weight) and also because parasites like flies and ticks are unable to get to any open wounds. It was pretty clear to me that the end was near for my old friend.

After a few days he got out of the water for a while and inadvertently strayed out of the park, even then he was quite tolerant of people who, thankfully, they did not tease him. He eventually did go back into the park.

Keeping him company was an old bull gaur, who was not in the best of health himself. This gaur had been observed coming out of the park and spending time next to the tusker. For the next two to three weeks these two were seen very close to each other and had seemed to have formed a bond of some sort. Maybe they understand each other's pain or suffering. I am not the type that usually gets sentimental about wildlife but this situation had forced me to react in unexpected ways.

The story does not have a happy ending, the tusker died in the river and his body was hauled out by the Forest Department using domesticated elephants. As his body was dragged out, the bull gaur came out of the Park and tried to get as close to the tusker as possible, utterly oblivious to the presence of humans. The people also did not bother him and watched him as he stood there. It was one of the most surreal moments of my life — an undeclared truce between man and beast — to mourn the dead and pay their last respects.

THE AMPHITHEATRE OF LIFE AND DEATH

Nature has this uncanny ability to catch us off guard, of surprising us when we least expect it. Just when we think that we have seen it all it pulls something out of its hat and makes us rethink everything that we thought we knew. It is this that keeps drawing us back time and time again. Sometimes I feel that one can spend a lifetime studying one small patch of forest and still, at the end of the day, feel that one has not progressed beyond the first few chapters. For a decade or so, Kabini was my patch of forest.

The backwaters of the Kabini needs no introduction as it is well known amongst wildlife enthusiasts both in India and abroad. An irrigation dam was built across the Kabini River in 1974, which resulted in the submergence of large tracts of forests and the creation of a huge lake, parts of which fall within the national park.

Every year during the summer months, the gates of the dam are opened to let water out to irrigate the crops downstream and as the waters bring life to the thirsty crops downstream, the levels in the reservoir dip and wide vistas open up. The resultant open plain supports an abundance of fresh grass more reminiscent of African savanna than tropical India. This unique micro-habitat has proved to be a boom for wildlife, providing fresh grass and water when the rest of the park is drying out.

This open plain, bisected by the Kabini now flowing in its original course, resembles a huge bowl with gently sloping sides. Gentle rolling hills provide a backdrop on three sides. During my time this bowl used to be ringed by giant bamboo. The bamboo has since flowered and died out, but it dominated the landscape when the incident I am about to narrate played out. Whenever I see this bowl the great Colosseum in Rome comes to mind. And much like the Colosseum here too the game of life and death is played out in front of a paying audience which is why I like to call it the amphitheater of life and death.

It was sometime in early 2010 when I first saw the family late one evening. It was a small family for an elephant family — two females and a calf. The calf was sleeping or resting among the boulders while the two females grazed quietly besides it. It was a peaceful scene and I spent a good part of the afternoon watching them from my boat. It was one of those beautiful moments that few are privileged to experience along the banks of the Kabini.

A few days later I chanced upon the family again and decided to spend some time with them. I was able to photograph them together as the calf suckled from his mother with his aunt staying close by. It was a typical elephant family moment and all seemed well with their world. However I did notice that the family seemed a bit too protective of the calf. Elephant families are extremely tight knit and are protective of each other especially of the young ones. What bothered me was the fact that elephant families are more at ease along the banks of the Kabini as they feel secure and safe here, this clearly was not the case with this particular family and it played on my mind.

The next day when I encountered them on the river bank they charged at my boat. This was rather unusual as they generally do not charge the boat. I was troubled because I do not like being charged by elephants, to me an elephant charge equates to failure. The failure to properly judge an elephant's private space and for a naturalist that is the ultimate failure. Encroaching onto an animal's private space can be disastrous and the consequences fatal. Needless to say, I was a bit down in the dumps the rest of the evening.

The family remained on the banks of the Kabini for the next few weeks and I would leave them alone as I knew that they did not wished to be approached as closely as the other elephants. It is always better to respect an animal's wishes especially if you want to observe them go about their daily lives. A wild animal at ease in your presence is the best endorsement of your skill as a naturalist.

A few days later I noticed the calf all alone. This was unusual as calves are never left alone. The two females had swum across the river to an island and were grazing there, effectively leaving the calf unguarded and exposed to danger. Surprised, taken aback and intrigued I decided to wait and watch, little knowing that I was about to witness something that would change my perception forever.

A jungle crow caught my attention; it was harassing the calf and seemed to be pecking it on its head. I scanned the calf's forehead with my binoculars and noticed that it had a series of large deep wounds on its head. The crow was attempting to pick the flesh from the wound.

The calf eventually came very close to the boat and started splashing the wound with water. It was obviously in a lot of pain and was using the water to try and get some relief. It even rubbed its wound against a tree stump for relief and finally exhausted, it lay down to rest. All this was happening a few meters away from the boat.

My attention was focused on the two females; I did not want a repeat of the previous incident. However I was in for a shock. All my previous experience with elephants, all the knowledge that I thought I had acquired was about to be turned on its head. The females were unconcerned. Those who have lived with elephants will realize the gravity of that last sentence. An elephant mother and aunt unconcerned about a calf? Impossible. I have seen an elephant mother and aunt spend days near the body of a stillborn calf. Their agony and pain was there for the entire world to see. It was one of the most painful experiences and I have watched a pack of wild dogs devour a deer, while its life ebbed away with each bite, more than once.

I turned the boat in the direction of the two females and this time they allowed me to approach closely without the least hint of aggression. This was a bit much for me and I subjected them to a critical examination. It was while doing so that I noticed a scar on the trunk of one of the females. It was an old wound that had completely healed but it was a nasty one.

I tried to piece together their story with the little evidence that I had ... that the family had been subject to a deadly assault was obvious. It was also fairly obvious that the calf was the target as its wounds were fresh and far worse. But who was or who were the perpetrators? Man? It seemed unlikely, only the foolish would attack an elephant calf with its family. Elephants migrate to the Kabini backwaters during this season and while doing so come into a lot of conflict with humans. Raiding of crop fields is, unfortunately, a grim reality. The wound on the adult female elephant's trunk could have been inflicted with a machete by someone from the safety of a machan but the wounds on the calf's head? They had to be inflicted from close range.

The only other plausible explanation that came to mind was a tiger attack. Tigers are known to attack and kill elephant calves and this could be one of those rare instances. The fact that this was a small family also led me to favour the tiger theory. The tiger would have been more circumspect if it was a larger herd. However I was not fully satisfied with either explanation. The wounds on the calf were very bad and I was not certain that a tiger could inflict such wounds; I have never seen an elephant calf kill.

The forest department was informed about the calf and they did come and rescue it but were unable to save its life. The official cause of death was recorded as a tiger kill.

The most troubling part about this entire episode was the behaviour of the two females. They seemed to have given up on the calf. I was unable to bring myself to accept this and to this day I am disturbed by it. For a long time I was unable to come up with a satisfactory explanation. Or maybe I was just not willing to consider or acknowledge it. It was one of those instances when nature confounds you, when you realise that nature can be extremely cruel. But who are we to judge? The females must have realised that the calf was doomed and that it was not worth investing any more time and effort on it. It's the only explanation but it turned what I have learnt and believed about elephants on its head.

I am penning this story after a gap of over ten years. During that time I have endeavored to find out if this behaviour had been recorded before and was able to find a couple of similar instances. The incident did shake my faith. The audience in the Colosseum enjoyed the spectacle of gore and death put up for them. I did not enjoy this.

A PREDATOR'S PARADISE

It was not long before I realised that there was something unique about the place that did not quite blend with what I had experienced before. In Kabini I regularly found tigers, leopards and wild dogs in the same areas, sharing space and seemingly coexisting. Conventional wisdom told me that this was not how it was meant to be. I mentioned this to some people but did not get a satisfactory explanation. To their mind, it was what the animals were used to.

Not satisfied, I decided to put it aside for the moment and got back to the daily grind. I was fortunate that the owner and my boss KP was himself extremely keen on wildlife and was also active in the conservation movement in the state. Thanks to that, I had the good fortune of interacting with eminent researchers and scholars from India and around the world. One such person was Dr K Ullas Karanth and I was able, with the help of his assistants, to get hold of some of his studies conducted in the Park; it must be mentioned here that in those days there was no mobile connectivity leave alone internet in Kabini and getting hold of any scientific information was difficult. As expected, within those papers I found the answers I was looking for. I will now attempt to cut through the jargon and explain the same to you. Rest assured what I am about to outline below is based on proper peer-reviewed scientific research and any errors are solely due to my misunderstanding them.

The Nagarhole National Park, of which Kabini is a part, has a large number of predators and the three major ones are the tiger, wild dog and leopard. As mentioned earlier these three major predators co-exist here in high densities due to a unique set of factors and circumstances.

To fully understand the relationship and dynamics between the predators we first need to look at their basic requirement — food or the herbivore density and the availability of prey species in the area. Without prey, it is impossible to have any predators and hence both the number and type of herbivores present play an important role. It is not just a question of numbers it also boils down to the kind of prey, for example, a forest inhabited only by hares cannot be expected to hold tigers as hares make too small a meal for them regardless of the number.

Nagarhole has a large number and variety of large herbivores (defined as weighing more than five kilos) and these include seven species of ungulates and two species of primates. Among these herbivores, the chital, sambar, gaur, wild pig, muntjac and the langur constitute almost the entire diet of the three. It is also interesting to note that all three, more or less, hunt the same species.

However when we further sub-divide them by body weight into large, medium and small, we find that the three predators have very distinct preferences. The average weight of prey killed by each worked out to 92 kg, 38 kg and 43 kg early showing the niche occupied by each predator.

The study also showed that there was species selectivity among the predators with gaur being preferred by tigers and wild pig being avoided by leopards and langurs being underrepresented among the wild dogs. Further tiger predation also showed a bias towards adult male chital, sambar and wild pig. Wild dogs were found to prey selectively on adult male chital while leopards avoided them. The studies showed that as there is a choice in Nagarhole, because of the availability of prey in the appropriate size class, the larger predators selectively kill larger prey which in turn facilitates co-existence.

Behavioural and hunting techniques as well as patterns play an important role in the relationship between these three predators. The study showed that wild dogs hunted almost always during the day probably because of their hunting method. They course or run down their prey and therefore find it easier to hunt during the day when visibility is good. Another reason is that they prey mainly on chital who are more active during the day.

Tigers and leopards were found to be more of nocturnal hunters thus there was some temporal (time) separation between them and the dogs. Leopards were also found to be relatively active during the day in comparison with tigers. This can be explained by the fact that leopards kill a relatively larger proportion of prey that are active during the day like the langur and chital. Even at night leopards were found to be more active than tigers. This was because they spend more time searching for prey due to the higher proportion of smaller nocturnal animals in their diet. However their activity pattern does not show any active avoidance of tigers by hunting at different times of the day.

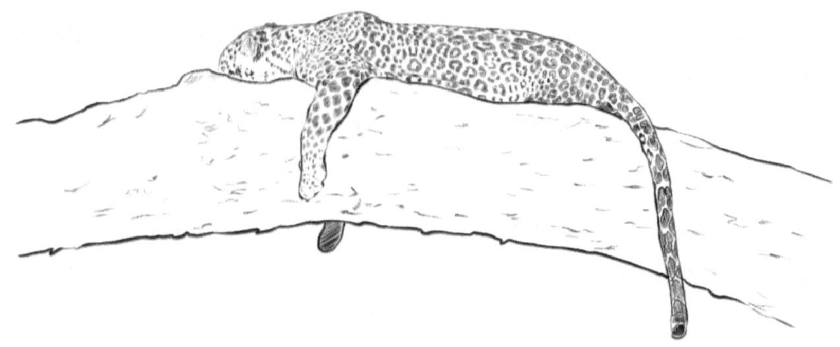

The studies also showed that there is no separation based on hunting areas selected by the three. All three attacked their prey close to habitat features where prey concentrated to feed or drink. But tigers killed their prey where the cover was significantly denser in comparison to leopards and most gaur (potentially dangerous) were attacked in the relatively open areas where visibility was higher. Leopards killed chital in more open areas than tigers as they have a greater ability for concealment in sparse cover.

Both leopards and tigers were found to drag their kills into cover, the dogs, however, did not drag their kills and any drag seemed incidental to the feeding process.

Tigers dragged their kills into dense to moderate cover but left some of their kills in the open, these being gaur were too heavy to carry. The leopard on the other hand dragged very few of their kills up into trees and also left a significant number in the open. Most wild dog kills were left in the open.

Field observations showed that leopards flee tigers and wild dogs by climbing trees. Tigers also appropriated wild dog and leopard kills. Wild dogs were observed scavenging tiger and leopard kills when they were away. In one instance the leopard returned to the kill later. On one occasion a tiger and leopard fed on kills less than 300 m apart without being aware of each other. On another occasion, a pack of wild dogs were 50 m away from a resting tiger again without either being aware of each other's presence. This showed that both tigers and wild dogs are socially dominant over leopards but all three share the same space. However tigers and leopards kill and eat wild dogs occasionally. The impression is that the need to defend kills does not play a significant role because of the dense cover and high tree density in Nagarhole.

It can be summarised that ecological factors such as availability of appropriate size prey, dense cover and high tree density are the reasons for the coexistence of these three in high densities in Nagarhole. Behavioural factors such as habitat preference, choice of hunting sites or social dominance, are of lesser importance in Nagarhole when it comes to predator densities.

I hope it made sense to you while it was eye-opening for me. A lot of water has flowed under the bridge since these studies were conducted and I left Kabini. The predators have become used to the safari vehicles and tigers especially, are seen more often. I am sure that tigers being less circumspect than before has, in turn, affected both leopard and wild dog behaviour. From what I see on social media, and there is a lot on social media, leopards are now mostly seen on trees — which, with tigers moving around with confidence, is not surprising. This was hardly the case during the decade or so I spent there, I saw most of my leopards walking on the ground. Well as they say change is the only constant and I guess it's time for another study — any takers?

KAKANKOTE KHEDDA

The elephant has been an integral part of Indian culture, history and religious belief since times immemorial. From ancient times till the recent past, it has played a significant role both as a vehicle of war and as a beast of burden. It is no wonder that the elephant has entered the Hindu pantheon in the form of Lord Ganesha, who is arguably the most popular deity in India. The elephant also figures prominently in other religions that originated in India namely Buddhism and Jainism.

Ancient Sanskrit literature is a rich source of information on the methods of capture and care for elephants. The sage Palakapya, who lived in what is now Orissa in the 5th century, is considered the founder of elephant lore as recorded in the Sanskrit classic the Gajashastra. The Ramayana also has references to elephant capture, vividly described by Valmiki. Scenes of elephant capture have been depicted on the walls of the Konark Temple in Orissa. In addition to the records in Sanskrit literature, both the Chola Kings of Tanjore and the Ahoms of Assam have left behind a large collection of elephant literature.

Western writers and commentators on India have left their own written accounts. They include Megasthenes in 200 BC, Strabo in 130 AD and Indicoplenstes in 600 AD. The European conquerors of India, the British, soon realised the importance of elephants in India and took over the business of elephant capture. They left detailed records on the methods used and attempted to standardis procedures for their capture, training and handling in captivity.

Sanskrit literature lists five methods for capturing wild elephants, one of which was the *khedda* method. Over a period of time each of these methods came to be associated with certain areas of the country.

The *khedda* method, associated with the eastern part of the country, was introduced with various modification to other parts of the country as well. The most famous of which was the Mysore State. Some of the most successful *khedda* operations were staged in the Kakankote State Forest, now part of the Kabini area of the Nagarhole National Park.

The first person, in the Mysore State, to try and capture elephants in this way was Hyder Ali, the father of Tipu Sultan, in the seventeenth century. He was unsuccessful and no further attempts were made. The British were the first to try again and an attempt by Colonel Pearson, a British Army officer, in 1867 also resulted in failure.

The next to try was another British officer, this time from the Canal or Irrigation Department, named GP Sanderson. He had no previous experience in capturing elephants, he was however interested and knowledgeable in the habits of wild elephants. After repeated representations which were supported by his superior, the Mysore Government in 1873 undertook to capture wild elephants and he was put in charge.

He was successful in his second attempt in 1874 at a place called Kardihalli. In 1875 he was put in charge of the British Elephant Catching establishment at Dhaka for a period of nine months. On his return from

Dhaka he adapted and perfected the *khedda* system in Mysore. He is said to have brought experienced elephant men from Dhaka who formed the mainstay of the operation. In time the Kuruba tribals of Mysore and others learnt the art of elephant driving.

After that *khedda* became a regular feature in the Mysore State. A total of 36 *kheddas* were conducted in Mysore till the last one in 1970–71.

The Kakankote forest, now the DB Kuppe Wildlife Range of Nagarhole National Park, became a favoured staging ground for the *khedda* and as many as twenty four were staged there. The Kakankote forest consists of tropical moist deciduous forest with a good amount of bamboo. They extended over large tracts and, along with the Begur forest, now part of the Bandipur National Park, on the opposite bank of the Kabini River were home to vast herds of wild elephants.

The Mysore *khedda* especially the Kakankote *khedda* (now part of the Kabini area of the Nagarhole National Park) were very different from the Assam *khedda*. The Mysore *khedda* were large undertakings which required a large number of men and *koonkis* (tame elephant trained for elephant catching). Wild elephant herds had to be driven in from long distances and were moved in stages and held when necessary in position until the exact time when they would be driven into the stockade in full view of distinguished guests.

This involved months of planning and preparation and large contingents of men and *koonkis*, as many as forty *koonkis* and a thousand men would be used. The size of the stockade would extend over five acres. The unique feature of a Kakankote *khedda* was the river drive which was first designed and carried out by GP Sanderson in honour of The Grand Duke of Russia during his visit to Mysore in 1891. In the river drive the elephants were driven across the Kabini into the stockade and this proved to be a popular spectacle with a special visitor's gallery being set up to allow people to witness the grand finale of a Kakankote *khedda*.

The only other elephant capturing operations that could compare with the Mysore *khedda* as a spectacle were those of Thailand. Here too the *khedda* method was of ancient origin and was staged every few years near the city of Ayuthia. It is interesting to note that the *kraal* method of capturing elephants as practiced in Sri Lanka is comparable to that of Mysore and Thailand.

Another aspect of the *khedda* was the Roping Operation. This involved moving the captured elephants out of the stockade and choosing individuals that were deemed suitable for training. *Koonkis* bearing their mahout and one additional person would enter the stockade. Paradoxically the movement of these *koonkis* among the captured and now very nervous and suspicious herd would have a calming effect on them. Once the herd had got used to the *koonkis* and calmed down somewhat, the mahouts would slowly and gradually start separating individual animals from the herd.

Two or more *koonkis* would 'sandwich' the separated individual and the second person seated behind the mahout would descend to the ground with ropes and hit the wild elephant's hind leg. This would make the elephant lift his foot off the ground and the person would slip a rope around it. The other end of the rope would be fastened to the *koonki*. Both hind legs would be bound and a third rope would be slipped over the captive's neck. Gradually and in stages the captive would be lead out of the stockade and fastened to a tree at an elephant camp specially established for this purpose.

One by one all the elephants would be separated and fastened with the exception of calves that were still nursing and so would be permitted to stay with their mothers. The Roping Operation was one of the most dangerous of all tasks associated with the *khedda* especially when females were separated from their calves that were already weaned. I don't have to describe the trauma and frenzy that would have ensued when this was done.

SABU – THE FIRST INDIAN STAR IN HOLLYWOOD

While the list of celebrities who attended the *khedda* is well known, what seems to have been forgotten is that the Mysore *khedda* also threw up the first Indian star in Hollywood. In 1935 Robert Flaherty arrived in Mysore to make a film called 'Elephant Boy' based on a story by Rudyard Kipling called 'Toomai of the Elephants' from his bestselling work *The Jungle Book*. The film was produced by the legendary producer Sir Alexander Korda.

The part of Toomai was played by a boy called Sabu. He was born in the Karapura village on the banks of the Kabini where there was a large elephant camp. The Kabini area was the hunting ground of the Maharaja of Mysore and a Royal hunting lodge was situated there (now known as the Kabini River Lodge).

Sabu was the son of a mahout and was raised among the elephants in the camp. His mother died early and legend has it that a female elephant rocked his cradle. His father died soon after and he was subsequently raised by the Mysore State.

The movie was shot in the forests along the banks of the Kabini and included a *khedda*, which was specially staged for the movie shoot. After location shooting, Sabu accompanied the unit to London to complete the film at the Korda's studio. After a while Sabu moved to Hollywood where he featured in various movies such as The Jungle Book, The Drum and The Thief of Baghdad. He returned to Mysore for a visit, driving a Cadillac, in 1952.

Sabu Dastagir, to give his full name, died in 1963 aged 39, of a heart attack at his Chatsworth CA home. He was survived by his wife, the former actress Marilyn Cooper, his son, Paul (singer, songwriter, producer, and guitarist) and his daughter, Jasmine. His funeral service was conducted at the Chapel of the Hills, Forest Lawn Memorial-Park Hollywood Hills. He was last seen in the Warner Bros. film *Rampage*.

DAY OF THE BARKING DEER

It started as the day of the barking deer as I saw three of them, in different locations, during the morning safari. I was even fortunate to have been able to capture them on film and was feeling quite pleased with myself. Of course, I would have had to wait to see how they would have come out as I had gone back to shooting with a film camera and one could never really tell — the glorious uncertainties of film.

My luck continued to hold in the evening, I had gone across the lake to the Kabini River Lodge to collect the safari permits, and as soon as I had them I received a call cancelling the safari. I had initially decided not to conduct the safari in the evening but I now found myself on the right side of the river with a permit in my hand but no guests. Since the permit was paid for and not refundable I did what any sane person, not that I make any claims on sanity, would do — I proceededwith the safari.

As is my wont when I am alone, I headed towards the loneliest part of the park — the Russell's Line. At the park gate, I took the right towards the Nainji Katte, a waterhole on Russell's Line. We surprised a herd of chital as they were proceeding towards the waterhole. They were perfectly silhouetted on an embankment near the waterhole. After taking a good look at us they proceeded on their way. Unfortunately they seemed to have already had a drink and so went away from the water. I switched off the engine and settled down to wait. I love waiting at this place primarily because it is not a very popular spot and hardly anybody frequents the area. This gives me the privacy I prefer. I take this opportunity to listen to the jungle sounds. It does not matter that I do not see anything as long as I can listen. That day too, the area was alive with bird calls and I enjoyed myself listing and waiting hopefully for an alarm call that never came.

After a while, I decided to move ahead to the open clearing where I was expecting to find grey jungle fowl feeding on the seeds of grass. But I had not bargained for the fact that the grass had dried up and so did not find them there as I had hoped. After a hasty consultation with Shabir, my driver, I decided to visit as many waterholes as possible. This would mean a fair bit of driving which was quite unlike me but I decided to go ahead.

At the entrance to Temple Road, there is a small waterhole that is so small that it has not been named, and it was here where we stopped again. A few green imperial pigeons were perched on a tree, a greater racquet-tailed drongo flew by, and a barking deer approached the waterhole with its typical halting gait. Barking deer are extremely shy and this one, which was a male sporting fine antlers, was very careful while approaching the water. It was aware of our presence and kept looking at us. It bounded away quickly after quenching its thirst.

After a while, we glimpsed a gaur moving behind a clump of bamboo, it was a female, and it was approaching the water. Another female with a very young calf followed it — less than three months old, as the white stockings, so typical of the gaur, had not yet been formed. I was very happy, as I had not seen gaur for a long time. Shortly after, a large bull gaur also stepped out and they went to the waterhole for a drink. I managed to get a photograph as they drank.

The bull suddenly stopped drinking and turned to look in the direction of the road behind him. After a while, I heard a Jeep approaching and before we knew it the gaur left the waterhole and disappeared from sight.

We now proceeded towards Greetal Kunji Kere as we wanted to avoid the Jeep. I would have preferred to wait at the waterhole a little while longer but I wanted to avoid the approaching vehicle. On the way to the Kere, we spied a Malabar Giant Squirrel on a tree and stopped a while to watch him as he scampered from branch to branch, tree to tree with the sunlight setting his beautiful maroon coat on fire. At the Kere, we saw a female elephant half-hidden behind a rise. She approached the water slowly and began to drink. I took a photo just to finish the roll as the light was rapidly fading. Leaving her to finish her drink, we drove away towards Somaniah Kere.

There we struck gold. A herd of elephants with two calves that were barely a week old. We spent the rest of the safari watching them.

LUCKY BREAK

I got lucky last week, I managed a safari on my own with no guests and it was like the old times. Determined to make the most of the opportunity, I decided to go and wait at a less frequented waterhole named Nainji Katte near the Russell's Line. On the way, I saw an elephant cross the road which I took as a good omen for elephants are my favourite animals. I reached the waterhole and parked the Jeep, letting the silence soak into me as the engine died.

This particular waterhole was home to a few families of jacanas and I was hoping to observe them as they went about with their daily routine. On the far side perched on a low stump, I spied a Brown fish owl. It just stood there surveying the waterhole and the two of us shared the silence, lost in our thoughts, two strangers coming together temporarily in silent contemplation.

I waited for about half an hour, during which time the owl decided to move on when I heard faint alarm calls of the chital coming from an open clearing that lay a little ahead of the waterhole. I knew the clearing well, the grass there should be seeding right about now and I was aware that it would in turn attract a lot of grey jungle fowl. I decided to drive on and, sure enough, I was not disappointed and settled down to watch them. Completely engrossed in gorging on the seeds, these generally shy birds came close to the Jeep allowing me to observe them at close quarters as they went about their business totally unconcerned by my presence — a rare treat indeed.

After a while, the alarm calls were repeated and I decided to drive another two hundred yards or so to where I thought the calls were coming from. The lure of an alarm call is just too tempting to resist. I drove on as quietly as possible and finally stopped close to a Nelli tree which was full of langurs. The langurs were silent and I realised that there were no predators around and should one show up they would surely see it. I, therefore, decided to spend some time with them as they are quite entertaining company. While waiting I heard a White-rumped shama, a well known Kabini songster, and was delighted as always with its call. After a while, a sambar doe walked out of the undergrowth behind the Jeep and stood watching me. She was a bit suspicious but not unduly alarmed. After assuring herself that I meant no harm, she slowly crossed the road and disappeared into the undergrowth. A flock of Plum-headed parakeets flew overhead.

As the langur seemed quite at ease I decided to move on, I wanted to spend some time near an old temple in the forest. On the way to the temple, I chanced upon an elephant mother and calf near a manmade salt lick. The salt lick was in an open clearing and they were grazing on the grass in the clearing. I stopped the Jeep and watched them as they grazed peacefully. An elephant with a calf is usually quite skittish but these two were completely at ease and they slowly moved closer and closer to the Jeep. I have often had grazing elephants come within touching distance from the vehicle. As long as you are quiet and can read their body language there is no real threat. To me, elephants at ease in my presence is the greatest compliment that I can ever receive as a naturalist.

Unfortunately for me, it was getting time to leave and I had no choice but to start the Jeep and drive towards the gate. On the way back I saw two wild boars and a herd of gaur with one large bull. Paradise Regained.

OF TEMPLES AND FORESTS

In ancient India, temples and forests have had a mutually beneficial relationship. From the days of yore, trees have been the focus of religious life for many people around the world and have been invested in all cultures with a dignity unique to their individual natures.

In myriad cases, the spirit of trees is personified, usually in female form. In India, tree nymphs appear in the form of the voluptuous Vrikshaka, and it is believed that the Brahma Daitya, the ghosts of Brahmans, live on fig trees, the pipal or the banyan, awaiting liberation or reincarnation.

Among the eight or so tree species considered sacred in India, these two varieties of fig are the most highly revered. Forests have been the lifelines of forest-dwelling communities since ancient times. One method for conserving this green resource was the creation of sacred groves, usually dedicated to a local deity.

A traditional means of biodiversity conservation, these groves can be considered the ancient equivalent of natural sanctuaries where all forms of living creatures are protected by a deity. No one is permitted to cut any tree or plant, kill animals and birds, or harm any form of life in this area.

Ancient Indian texts include several references to sacred groves, including Kalidaasa's Vikramorvawsiyam. Temple forests in India have served many spiritual and religious purposes.

Temples, beyond their religious significance, played a crucial role in protecting forests. It's no wonder that every Protected Area in India is graced by the presence of an ancient temple. Kabini, for instance, is home to two such temples, a testament to the harmonious coexistence of spirituality and nature.

The first is a Tribal Temple located near a safari road named after it — the Temple Road. This temple, built of granite slabs, is now abandoned and almost covered by vegetation. It is one of the most spiritual places I have ever visited.

The other one is the more famous Mastigudi temple, which is now submerged by the construction of the Kabini dam. The deity is Ganesha, who is carved onto the face of a single rock. The temple is visible during the summer when the waters recede.

Today, the sight of wild elephants grazing beside the image of Ganesha can only be witnessed in Kabini. It serves as a poignant reminder of a traditional means of biodiversity conservation that has been tragically lost. This ancient practice is a testament to the deep respect for nature in ancient India.

MASTIGUDI

The Mastigudi temple, situated on the banks of the Kabini river in Balle Shibira, is dedicated to the Goddess Mastamma. Mastamma means 'the great wife' (Maha + Sati + Amma), a name of Goddess Parvati and 'Gudi' means temple. It stood next to the old Mysore — Malabar road and has since been submerged after the construction of the Kabini dam.

While the temple is dedicated to the Goddess Mastamma, the main idol is that of Lord Ganesha. Carved on the face of a large rock it is stunningly beautiful in its simplicity. Standing next to Lord Ganesha is the Goddess Mastamma. Every year during the summer, when water is released for irrigation from the reservoir, the idols rise like a phoenix above the receding waters. The temple structure has been destroyed totally and only the idols remain.

The temple of Goddess Mastamma or Goddess Masti (as she is popularly known) is believed to be endowed with powerful spiritual powers and devotees passing through the forests would seek her blessing and protection for their journey.

In 1973 the famous kannada movie 'Gandhada Gudi' was filmed in these forests. The megastar Dr Rajkumar, who starred in the film, would visit the temple everyday to seek the Goddess's blessings and protection.

The film was not without incident, during the climax the gun used by the villain was fired accidently wounding Dr Rajkumar. It is believed that Dr Rajkumar escaped with his life due to the protection offered by the Goddess. In fact, when the movie 'Gandhada Gudi — Part 2' was planned in 1993, Dr Rajkumar insisted that his son and hero of the film take the blessings of Goddess Masthamma before commencing shooting.

In 2016 in an unfortunate incident of a stunt gone wrong, two actors lost their lives on the sets of a movie titled 'Masti Gudi'. It is believed that had they taken the blessings of the Goddess Mastigudi, the unfortunate tragedy would have been averted.

THE LOST TEMPLES OF KABINI

A nondescript path, barely visible to the untrained eye, snakes its way through the overgrown undergrowth of a much-neglected Oil Palm grove. The path drops off down a gentle incline toward the river and there under the branches of an ancient tree lie the ruins of the lost temples of Kabini.

Two walled enclosures situated side by side house one temple each — to the left lies a structure in terminal decline, dwarfed by gnarled trees and vegetation — the Gopalaswamy Temple. To the right and in close proximity, in a high walled enclosure guarded by fierce looking figurines, lies the much plainer looking Padmavati Temple. Two shrines of two distinct faiths that once vied for supremacy lie peacefully next to each other. One can almost feel the underlying tensions that must have existed between the two.

Nothing ignites an archaeologist's imagination like the prospect of a lost city and right here seemingly in the middle of nowhere and hidden in plain site lie two temples that time seems to have forgotten. An Indiana Jones moment, depending on your choice of vintage, if there ever was.

The Gopalaswamy temple dedicated to Lord Vishnu is built in traditional fashion — granite superstructure upon which rests a brick gopuram. A pillared entrance leads onto a long hall, the floor of which has been dug up — treasure hunters perhaps? Carved pillars lead to a dark room the entrance to which is flanked by two figures. On the top of the entrance is an intricately carved image of Lord Vishnu resting on Sheshnaga or Adishesha.

Another small square granite shrine is located at one corner of the enclosure, surrounded by vegetation and made inaccessible by it. As one circles the main temple, one notices the fish emblem, closely associated with Lord Vishnu, carved on the outer walls.

The Padmavati temple, on the other hand, is a much simpler and more plain structure almost in keeping with the comparatively austere nature of Jainism. Once you enter the walled compound, the main shrine is just a few feet away. As one enters the shrine one is greeted by white washed pillars. Much plainer than the Gopalaswamy temple, these pillars lead to a smaller room that houses a chest of drawers with a modern-day sculpture of the Mahavira. An old brass bell hangs forlornly from the ceiling.

It is clearly evident that the temple is used occasionally for prayer, though one could not tell from the outside. The compound is overgrown and the outside of the temple is in a sad state of repair. The inside, on the other hand, is well swept, whitewashed and tidy. One wonders about the identity of the caretakers, for while the area was once a stronghold of Jainism, there are hardly any practitioners left.

Enquiries about the antecedents of both temples and the mystery caretakers draw a blank, the locals seem rather ambivalent towards them. There is surely a story lurking in the undergrowth somewhere perhaps a mystery to be solved or a nugget of history to be unearthed. A job best left to a better man.

THE LEGEND OF KARAPURA

Karapura village, located on the banks of the river Kabini, has an interesting connection to the Ramayana. While the incident is not specifically mentioned in the Ramayana, a local legend (called the legend of Karapura) about Luv and Kush, the sons of Sita and Rama, establishes the connection between the two.

A little while after Rama's triumphant return to Ayodhya, he banished his wife Sita from his kingdom. We are all familiar with the story of her taking refuge in Valmiki's ashram and raising her two children Luv and Kush and the subsequent reunion with Rama.

According to the Karapura legend, after being banished by Ram, Sita was forced to wander the forests with her children Luv and Kush. This narrative differs significantly from the Ramayana that we are familiar with, for there Sita takes refuge in Valmiki's ashram where she raises her two sons.

During her wanderings, tired and hungry, Sita and her children take refuge under a tree. The children, as most hungry children are wont to, start pestering her to provide them with food. Sita then spies a flickering light in the distance and instructs the children to wait quietly till she returns with some food.

Sita moves towards the light which happened to be coming from a temple. Upon reaching the temple she is taken in by the priest, surprised at seeing a single woman wandering in the jungle during the night. Intrigued, he engages her in conversation which results in considerable delay as her story was both long and fascinating. At the end of her narrative and upon realising the lateness of the hour, the priest suggests that since Sita is herself nearing exhaustion, she should rest awhile at the temple while he would go with some food and fetch the children.

Upon arriving at the tree where the children were waiting for their mother, he was harangued by demands to take them to their mother. The priest comforts the children and promises them that if they behave themselves and eat the food that he had brought for them, he would take them to meet their mother.

The legend lives on in Karapura and the tree where the children took refuge (or its progeny) still stands today. There is a small makeshift shrine at its base. The original temple was sadly submerged during the construction of the Kabini Dam but a new temple was built as a replacement and occupies pride of place in the village today.

Every year, on a particular date, two children from the village dress up as Luv and Kush and after a series of religious ceremonies conducted at the tree shrine during the night, are taken in procession from the tree to the temple where they are symbolically reunited with their mother.

And thus, the legend of Karapura is passed on from one generation to another, not in a written form, but by the observance of an annual ritual.

HERO STONES

Memorial stones erected during ancient times in memory of a hero who martyred his life for a noble cause are called Hero Stones (Viragal in Kannada). These Hero Stones are found in many parts of Southern India.

The Hero Stones found in Karnataka are usually five feet tall granite stones, some of them being over a thousand years old. The landscape of Karnataka is liberally dotted with these stones that are a unique combination of art, poetry and historical fact and give us valuable insights into the fascinating times that our forebears lived in.

An archetypal Hero Stone has sculptures in three panels — the lower most is a depiction of the heroic deed, the middle one shows the Hero as a martyr being carried to heaven and the topmost depicts the Hero or Veera at Kailasa (Abode of Lord Shiva). It was believed that the spirit of the Hero resided forever in the Hero Stone, bestowing benefactions on the community. The spirit was dreaded, loved, adored and worshipped and was considered the saviour of the community.

There was a well laid down procedure for the erection of these Hero Stones. The first stage was the selection of a suitable stone for the memorial. The villagers would go to a nearby site to obtain a stone and after careful selection, usually from a rock, would sprinkle water over the stone while reciting a prayer to ensure that all the spirits that had been inhabiting the place may depart so that the stone could be acquired for the memorial.

The second stage involved the offering of flowers, incense and the praising of the stone, for it was "the stone" that was going to carry the name and fame of the great hero. The stone would then be quarried and transported to the village to the accompaniment of music and dance.

The third stage involved the stone being soaked in clean water for a number of days or for a specified period of time. It was held that since the stone had been exposed to the vagaries of weather, it was desirable that it be immersed in water.

The hero's figure was then carved and his exploits inscribed on the stone, after which it was ceremoniously placed in an appropriate place — usually on the outskirts of the village. A great food offering was then made and finally the Hero was praised and prayers were offered for the bestowal of prosperity on the village community.

It has been noted that in the construction of later Hindu temples the process of the selection of a stone for carving the image of a god, the carving of the image, the consecration and other rites are the same as those for the erection of these memorial stones.

Some Hero Stones bear inscriptions explaining the event and the name of the hero. Based on the script used in the inscription, archaeologists are able to date the period of the Hero Stone. These Hero Stones are very important records that lead to an understanding of the social and cultural milieu of this period in South India.

There is a Hero Stone in Kabini that clearly conforms to the above description. It depicts the Hero slaying a larger than life animal, probably a tiger.

BHIMANKOLLI

The people of Karnataka are familiar with the epic of Male Mahadeshwara. Lord Mahadeshwara is the family god of the Soligas and other tribals who live in the Male Mahadeshwara Hills of Karnataka. There is a temple dedicated to Lord Mahadeshwara there which is an important place of pilgrimage. Historical evidence suggest that the Saint Mahadeshwara lived during the 15th century and came to the Male Mahadeshwara Hills, riding his Vahana or vehicle — a tiger also known as Huli Vahana. He performed a number of miracles around the hills to protect the people and saints living there. It is believed that he continues to perform penance in the temple's Garbha Gudi in the form of Linga.

The epic of Male Mahadeshwara describes the life and miracles of the Saint. It is divided into seven parts and is sung by pilgrims on their way to the annual fair on the Male Madheshwara Hills. The professional singers of this epic are called 'Devara Guddaru' (God's children) and 'Kamsaleyavaru' (those singers who keep time with 'Kamsale' — bronze cymbals).

On the banks of the Kabini River, not far from the resort lies the Bhimanakolli Temple dedicated to Lord Mahadeshwara. This is a modern structure built after the original was submerged when the Kabini Dam was built. Remains of the original temple can be seen when the waters of the reservoir recede during the summers. Bhimanakolli and its surrounding areas, now known as the Kabini area, is considered to be the birthplace of Lord Mahadeshwara. The Bhimanakolli Temple is not as well known as the temple in the Male Mahadeshwara Hills and the fact that this is the birth place of the Saint is also not widely known.

In the first part of the epic, which narrates the birth of Lord Mahadeshwara, this connection is clearly articulated. I quote from the epic as documented by K Keshavan Prasad and translated by CN Ramachandran and LN Bhat.

And sat in the hollow of a neem tree-
Of Halagappa, a Shepard by caste,
Living in the village of Bhimanakolli,
Of Magga Maralli Heggadedevanakotte.

The villages of Magga and Maralli are situated on the opposite bank of the river where they were relocated following the submergence of the original site. HD Kote is now the Taluk headquarters.

The Charmer of the ninth incarnation,
Who was in the hollow of the neem tree,
Thought: if I sit here, I can't save the world.
Then he entered the house of Halagappa,
The house that has twelve pillars,
And he went inside the house the Charmer,
And manifested himself there as a golden anthill.
When the golden anthill arose in the inner yard,
Halagappa and Muddamma, his wife, grew worried.

They took it to be a bad omen and tried to consult astrologers but could find no one to help them. The Charmer then appeared before them in guise of a Brahmin and told them that there was no bad omen, that the Charmer had come to them as a family deity and that they should worship him and give up their home. They then carried all their household things to the back of their house and built a small hut for themselves and in the morning took their bath and milked their cow and poured the milk over the anthill.

The story now takes a strange twist.
Then the Charmer of charmers,
Who was inside in the form of a small linga,
Thought thus: for the first time since I left Kailash,
I have had milk ablutions. From now on,
I should ameliorate the world.
But first I should get a festival
From this Halagappa and then begin my onward journey _
With these thoughts, to Magga, Maralli and Bhimananakolli,
In all these three villages
He caused a great famine — the Charmer

It was a terrible famine and the people of the three villages had to survive by eating all the grain they had stored as seed for sowing. When the rains came they had no seeds for sowing, except for Halagappa who had one granary of Ragi. He promises the villagers seeds after sowing his field. He proceeds to sow his field along with his son. However, as he sowed there arose small Lingas on his footprints.

All the people are hungry in the village
Whatever I sowed
You have turned into a Linga — he said.
Then the Charmer got a new name.
What was that name?
Linga in the temple, and
Linga around the temple.
O Mahadeva of the northern region.
You are born as Linga.
Laying down the basket of seeds on the eastern balk,
And having prostrated himself to the mother earth,

He said — my son, go on with your ploughing,
I will return to the field.
After I measure out Ragi
To the villagers to sow — so saying,
Halagappa then came to the village,
And gave away Ragi for all for sowing.
Then he returned to his field and finished his own sowing.
Then the Charmer of all charmers
Entered the dream of Halagappa,
And said: Look here, Gowda,
You are honest people, both husband and wife.
All of you of the three villages,
Magga, Maralli and Bhimanakolli,
Come together once a year during Shivrathri,
And in the name of Bhimanakolli Madappa,
Organize a fair in his name,
He departed from Bhimanakolli — Mahadeva.

The fair is organised by all three villages to this day. There is a further modern-day addition to the story. It seemed that there was a certain gentleman who used to do the lighting arrangements for the fair and suffered from stomach ulcers. He made a vow that if he got cured he would not charge the temple for his services. He did get cured and to this day his son continues to do the lighting arrangements for the fair.

PAPA JOHN: THE LIVING LEGEND

The jungles of Kabini have many legends associated with them, and one of them was a 'Living Legend' — Colonel John Felix Wakefield, lovingly called 'Papa' by all his friends, colleagues, guests, and probably all his 'friends in the jungle' too. Papa, aged 95, bid his final adieu to the one place he loved to live in and single-handedly placed it on the world tourism map: Kabini. Kabini will never be the same after the sad demise of the great man.

Born in Bihar in 1916, Papa's intimate relationship with wildlife began during his early years under the guidance of his father. After spending six years in England engaged in studies, Papa returned to where his heart lay: India.

He first worked as Manager of the Tajpur Estate at Bijnor. In 1941, he began his career in the Army, serving in various capacities until

1955. He was involved in the Jungle Training Division and the Burmese operations ending in Rangoon. He held the rank of Colonel in the Civil Affairs Services in Burma.

Yet, the allure of the jungle was too strong to resist. In 1967, Papa made a life-altering decision, transitioning from a successful career in the army to the world of wildlife tourism. This journey culminated in the establishment of a joint venture in Kabini in 1978, a move that would forever link his name with the place. The venture is better known as the Kabini River Lodge and, by extension, Jungle Lodges & Resorts.

Papa will always be remembered for his generosity and hospitality. He could be found every evening in his verandah sitting in his chair sipping his preferred poison — Famous Grouse whiskey. He had an endless store of stories and would enjoy sharing them with his many guests.

The bar in the Kabini River Lodge has been renamed in his honour, a gesture that he would wholeheartedly approve of. Rest in peace, Papa. Kabini misses you.

When I started to take a keen interest in wildlife, I also began to discover many people who would capture my imagination through the books they wrote about their adventures. Many of these were their shikar reminiscences, hunting down man-eaters and wildlife in general. One of the authors who stood out for me was Billy Arjan Singh. His accounts of his life on his farm called Tiger Haven really captivated me and I ended up reading all his books. Billy is also the legend responsible for setting up Dudhwa National Park.

His influence on me can be judged by the fact that I named my daughter after a tigress that he hand reared and reintroduced into the wild – Tara. I even managed to get a signed copy of his book Tiger Haven as my mother worked in a bookshop owned by one of his close friends.

One morning in Kabini I received a message from KP, my boss, in Bangalore asking me to go to the Kabini River to meet Papa John as there was some talk of the FD stopping the safaris due to some unfathomable reason. In those days there was no mobile network in Kabini and we had a temperamental landline so him getting through to Kabini was a minor miracle of sorts. I had just returned from the morning safari and headed straight to the Kabini River Lodge. My wife Gowri joined me as it was an opportunity to meet Papa. I must mention here that Papa had a soft spot for Gowri since he used to work for her family many moons ago.

We knew where to find Papa as it was breakfast time and he would be seated at his special table – I called it the high table as it overlooked the rest of the Gol Ghar or dining area. Only select guests would be invited to share the table with him. That morning I noticed that the table was unusually full. On seeing us he unhesitantly asked us to join him and we dutifully sat down – as I have said before he was very fond of Gowri. Seated next to him was an elderly gentleman with a walking stick.

After a few minutes of polite conversation he turned to me and gestured at the elderly gent with the stick, said in a casual manner – Vikram, meet Billy.

There is only one Billy and I just looked at him too stunned to say anything. Papa then introduced the person on my right – it was the owner of the bookshop, Billy's friend and my mother's old boss. I quickly introduced myself to him and we spent some time chatting about Calcutta and the old days. This helped break the ice and Gowri and I then engaged Billy in conversation – the FD and all associated problems were promptly forgotten.

After a while I excused myself to go and fetch all my copies of Billy's books which I wanted him to sign. He, very kindly, invited us to join him at his cottage on our return. I got all the books and we spent another hour in his company. He was quite pleased when I told him that I had named my daughter after his tigress and showed him the book he had signed in 1979.

The author Duff Hart Davis has penned a biography of Billy aptly named *Honorary Tiger*. Billy believed that the Tiger of Dudhwa considered him one of their own and had bestowed upon him the status of an honorary tiger.

It was an honour indeed to have met and broken bread with the Honorary Tiger. Billy passed away a few years later.

LOOKING BACK

The meeting with Billy Arjan Singh put me in a reflective mood and got me looking back on my wildlife journey, so to speak. My interest was sparked in boarding school, which has an ethos of outdoor sports including hunting and natural history (collecting eggs and feathers). It must have been in the year 1978 that I had stumbled upon a book called *The Wild Life of India* by EP Gee. My mother used to work in a bookshop, and that's where I had found it.

In 1999 my wife Gowri had presented me with another copy for my birthday (she had no idea that I already had a copy lying in my mother's house), and a few days ago, I reread it as I had run out of reading material. A full thirty years had passed since I first read it, and I thought it would be interesting to note the changes that have taken place in our wildlife landscape over my lifetime.

EP Gee was a British tea planter who had decided to make India his home after independence. He had worked for Octavius Steel & Co and as fate would have it, I joined the same organisation as a tea planter in 1993.

We are all familiar with the expression "there were forty thousand tigers in India" at the turn of the century. That figure is now treated as sacrosanct. Well, it was EP Gee who came up with that figure and he had used an educated guess to arrive at it. It goes to show that one needs to be careful about what one publishes, as after some time it is taken as a historical fact.

The forward to the book, which was first published in 1964, was written by Jawaharlal Nehru and it makes for an inspired reading. I present below a few excerpts.

"Wildlife? That is how we refer to the magnificent animals of our jungles and to the beautiful birds that brighten our lives. I wonder sometimes what these animals and birds think of man and how they would describe him if they had the capacity to do so. I rather doubt if their description would be very complimentary to man. In spite of our culture and civilization, in ways man continues to be not only wild but more dangerous than any of the so – called wild animals.

In India, perhaps even more than in other countries, there is this difference between precept and practice. In no country is life valued in theory so much as in India, and many people would even hesitate to destroy the meanest or the more harmful of animals. But in practice we ignore the animal world. We grow excited about the protection of the cow. The cow is one of the treasures of India and should be protected. But we imagine we have done our duty by passing some legislation. This results not in the protection but in much harm to it as well as to human beings. Cattle are let loose and become wild and become a danger not only to crops but to human beings. They deteriorate and the very purpose for which we value the cow is defeated."

I think he really hit the nail on the head.

Now, coming back to EP Gee. One of the book's highlights that is now of personal interest is a description of his visit to Bandipur and Periyar in 1950. He describes Bandipur as a 22 sq mile sanctuary and hopes that it gets extended as there are enough forests to do so. We all know that this in fact did happen. He also records that he saw over five hundred chital near the rest house. This bit of information stuck in my mind, and during my first trip to Bandipur in 1979, I eagerly looked forward to counting chital near the rest house. We all know that the number of chital near the rest house is now much lower. He also mentions visiting Mudumalai and seeing a lot of gaur in 1961. This was much before the outbreak of foot-and-mouth that decimated the gaur population in the south.

In 1960 he visited Periyar and recorded that he saw a large number of elephants and gaur from a boat. He also mentions a few large tuskers. Sadly we know what a circus Periyar has turned into now. In 1950, when he first visited, there was no food in the rest house in spite of the three months' notice that he had given them! That seems to be the only thing that has improved in Periyar.

He talks about wild buffalo being present in west and south Orissa in addition to the adjoining areas of Andhra and Madhya Pradesh. These no longer survive.

In Jaldapara, another of my stamping grounds, he mentions a population of forty rhinos. Well, the rhinos are still there and holding their own.

He writes about his efforts to persuade the Government of Bhutan to set up a sanctuary adjoining the Manas Sanctuary in India. Manas was then only 105 sq miles. However he failed to receive a response from the Government of Bhutan. We know that this has now happened, but the Bodo agitation wrecked Manas in India. With consistent effort Manas is now recovering, and the Bodos themselves are involved in its protection, which is a remarkable turnaround.

I recently met Kampa Borgoyary, the Deputy Chief of the Bodoland Territorial Council, and he informed me that the protection and rejuvenation of Manas was a question of Bodo pride and that they would significantly increase the size of the park. This has now been done.

EP Gee supposedly discovered the Golden Langur in Manas in 1953. As he points out in the book, he was indeed the first person to film them, and as a tribute to his endeavours, they are named after him — the Presbytis gee.

I could go on and on, but I really think you need to read the book. His best is a description of Kaziranga and Nehru's visit to it. He mentions that Nehru's daughter accompanied her father (does not mention her name). Little did he realise that if it had not been for her, we would have lost all our wildlife. Kaziranga was the first sanctuary I visited sometime in 1973-74, and one can say that it's where it all began for me, though my interest in wildlife had started much later. I still have vague memories of riding an elephant in the pouring rain and watching the rhinos. I also remember being turfed out of the Forest Department's rest house in the evening as a 'high official' had suddenly decided to visit. I guess some things never change.

I was inspired to take up wildlife photography, which I think was a natural progression, as hunting was no longer possible. It might come as a shock to the present generation but hunting was seen then as much of a passion as wildlife photography is today.

Some of the people whose exploits with the camera inspired me are FW Champion, Jim Corbett, and M Krishnan. I hope one day to be as good as them. For those who are not acquainted with these gentlemen, allow me to provide you with a brief introduction, for each deserves a book to himself.

FW Champion was a British forest officer who, instead of shooting with a rifle, which was the norm in those days, chose to photograph wildlife, and that too at night with a trip wire laid out to trigger the camera. His set-up (built and designed completely by himself) was the first camera trap. Champion was, in all probability, the first wildlife photographer of India.

Jim Corbett requires no introduction. He was inspired by FW Champion's photographs in his books *With a camera in Tiger Land* and *Jungle in Sunlight and Shadow*. He wanted to do one better and chose to shoot with a cine camera. He used an 8 mm camera but soon discovered that the 'whirring' disturbed the wildlife. To overcome the problem, he created a small waterfall in a jungle stream to drown out the sound made by the camera. This proved successful, and he records, in his usual dry and direct manner, that he managed to film six tigers and that one of them was a white tiger! I believe the footage is with the British Library.

M Krishnan was a freelance writer and photographer who came to the art late. He took up photography at the age of forty and produced some of the most breathtaking photographs of Indian wildlife. Besides being a photographer, he was also a great writer of natural history. His fortnightly column in The Statesman newspaper in Calcutta titled "Country Notebook" ran for a record 46 years with the last column appearing on 18 February 1996, the day he died.

WHERE IT ALL BEGAN

Now that I have got into a reflective mood allow me to bore you, dear reader, with a few more nuggets from the past. My first real encounters with wildlife began when I got a job as a tea planter. Yes, I started my working life as a tea planter in the southern Indian state of Kerala.

It was a huge leap of faith as I was not only unfamiliar with the area but also with the language. Talk about going out of one's comfort zone but that's the confidence or foolhardiness that goes hand in hand with youth.

After a couple of eventful years I moved to the Duars of North Bengal or the 'Empire's Edge' as I like to call it. It's that sliver of land that connects the north-eastern states of India with the mainland. Only 30 km wide and 350 km in length it shares borders with Bhutan, Nepal and Bangladesh. It should come as no surprise that it is one of the most militarised zones in India.

In early 1988 I started my career as a tea planter in the Wayanad district of Kerala. Having spent most of my time in Rajasthan, the countryside I was exposed to was predominantly brown in colour, and the lush green countryside of Kerala fascinated me. Even though I arrived in the middle of a drought, I found the area to be incredibly green. My Manager kept on about how dry it was, and for the life of me, I could not understand what he was talking about.

When the monsoon arrived, it was a shocking experience. I had never been exposed to so much rain before, and I remember it going on for thirty days nonstop. I don't think I was dry most of the time, and even now, I don't enjoy getting wet.

However there were some good areas where I could have some fun. My old school and college friend Karan had also joined the same company, and we ended up sharing the same bungalow.

Above the estate was a mosaic of open grassland and shola forests, which acted like a magnet for us, and we spent a lot of our weekends exploring the area. We would ride our Bullet motorcycles as far up the hill as possible, and then, leaving the bikes, we would proceed on foot. It was great fun.

The hilly terrain and the endless expanse of grass was new for us, and the pockets of Shola forests in between was something we had never imagined could exist. While the wildlife was a little thin on the ground, we did have some exciting moments, especially when we came across a raging wildfire. The entire hillside had been burned, and the flames were still smouldering when we reached.

In 1989 I was transferred to a tea estate in Gudalur Taluk of Tamil Nadu, close to the Kerala border. It was quite a small estate, as estates go. I was the only executive apart from the Manager. The Manager was a bit of an ass, and we did not get along; he was more interested in spending time away from the property. As a result I was more or less left to my own devices and decided to make the most of it. It was quite easy to avoid contact, and both of us scrupulously did so.

Right along the border of the property was a dense jungle with a small tribal colony between it and the property. In that colony lived an elderly man who used to work on the estate. I did not pay much attention till the day he was brought to the estate hospital with a bleeding scalp. He had stumbled upon a bear and had was mauled. Under the prevalent laws in force, he was eligible for full and free medical treatment. He, however, refused and went back to the colony. Then resurfaced after a while, completely cured.

It was then that I decided to take a closer look. After talking to him and my field officer, Ponappa, I realised that what I took to be a jungle was, in fact, a coffee plantation that had been abandoned after a coffee blight in the early 1900s. The plantation was part of our property and under my jurisdiction.

That was all I needed. I now spent most of my time exploring the area. The plantation had reverted to its natural state and stretched all the way to the Mudumalai Wildlife Sanctuary, with which it shared a boundary.

Within this abandoned estate, there was a wealth of wildlife, and I spent a lot of time learning how to track them with the help of Kullan, the old man. He showed me huge rosewood trees deep inside, the remains of the old Manager's bungalow and an old temple where his people used to pray. He also told me that the youngsters in the tribal colony had no interest in the old way of life and did not even know the location of the temple.

One evening I had sent the estate tractor and trolley into the old plantation to pick up a load of soil we had collected earlier in the day. The soil was to be used for our nursery. The work got delayed, and it was dark by the time the tractor returned. We decided to park the vehicle in the factory and unload it the next day. As we stopped and got down, we all froze in our tracks. A baby elephant had followed the tractor, and nobody had noticed till now. The baby elephant was young, maybe a few months old; it reached up to my waist. How and why it had followed us, I still don't know.

What to do? Ponappa and I decided to call Kullan. He duly arrived. We now had a council of war. Finally we decided to hand over the baby to the Forest Department at Mudumalai, where they had an elephant camp. A man was dispatched to the police station to report the fact over their wireless.

In the meantime we decided to feed the baby some milk. Ponappa was a huge, burly fellow. He held onto one side, and I held onto the other. Kullan lifted the trunk, and the baby took one step back. Both Ponappa and I were thrown to the ground. The baby had incredible strength.

We then decided that the best thing was to get the baby to Mudumalai at the earliest. We got the estate lorry, and Kullan got the baby inside. We then drove to Mudumalai and handed him over to the department. Sadly the baby did not survive as it was too young.

I also encountered a young leopard that got stuck in a freshly ploughed paddy field! But that's another story.

A NIGHT IN THE DUARS

Let me now jump about ten years to the Duars of Bengal. I am now on my second stint in an estate called Sylee.

Sylee is known in the Duars as the hotbed of man-elephant conflicts. Every year elephants kill an average of ten people and damage buildings worth a couple of lakhs. No one records the value of crops lost.

My wife Gowri and I were returning from a friend's place at 2 am. After getting home, I was woken up by a group of workers in a tractor coming to tell me of an elephant damaging homes. This was quite normal, and I asked them to take shelter in the factory as I was not in the mood to chase elephants at that hour.

Early the following day I went to the labour lines to check as I had a feeling that things were not quite right. Besides, I felt a little guilty about not responding during the night. There was chaos. About forty houses had been destroyed and three people had been killed. The bodies were unrecognisable as bodies. Pieces of meat and bone were all that was left. One body was strewn over twenty feet. Worse was to follow.

The workers had fled to the Chel Club in the tractor and to the club, I went. The first thing I saw was the tractor wrapped around the gatepost. The elephant had completely smashed it. I went to the front door of the club and nearly threw up. The elephant had caught one man outside the club and had smashed him against the wall in full view of the people hiding in the club, including his wife and children. He had matted hair, as some of our tribal workers were fond of having, and pieces of his scalp were dangling from the wall.

There was no sign of the body. I followed the blood trail and found the body thrown into some tea bushes. The rage of the elephant could be judged by the fact that he had dragged the body a fair distance before flinging it across a fence.

After a while, my friend Rajan reached the club. His division was about twelve km from the main estate and in a straight line as the crow flies from the club. He had a tale of his own. About twenty houses were destroyed, and four people were killed in his division. It was the worst night for Sylee.

The aftermath was difficult to handle as the entire labour force was up in arms. After the dust had settled, we monitored any reports of further incidents, and none were reported for a couple of weeks. The animal had obviously calmed down, and there were no reports of a lone elephant causing damage.

This incident was the worst case of man-elephant conflict that had ever occurred in the Duars until then. The famous elephant whisperer Parvati Barua visited Sylee, and it was a great learning experience as she reconstructed the events by studying the tracks and signs.

According to her reconstruction of the scene (largely confirmed by the people involved that night), a herd of elephants entered the Chel labour line from the Gorubathan side as they usually do. They then proceeded to feed in the kitchen gardens (labour lines in Duars are like large villages, with most houses having small kitchen gardens where vegetables are grown). The herd was peaceful and did not cause any damage to the houses.

After about an hour or so, when the herd had gradually made its way to the centre of the line, one animal went berserk. One could clearly ascertain the exact spot from where this particular animal's behaviour changed.

It was evident that something drastic had happened at this spot, but everybody was tight-lipped and refused to confirm or deny anything. We followed the trail all the way to the club and beyond, and the following story unfolded.

The herd seemed to have dispersed after this individual went berserk and was left behind. The matriarch, however, doubled back to check but could not calm things down. This individual then proceeded to Rajan's division and continued with the mayhem. It finally seems to have crossed over and disappeared into the forest beyond.

A few weeks later, a team from CNN visited us, and thanks to my interaction with Parvati Barua, I could expertly guide them and reconstruct the events of the fateful night. The episode was broadcast in the US.

I remained in Sylee for another two years. One day, in an unguarded moment, one of the residents of the line confessed to having thrown a burning blanket on the elephant that fateful night — his house was at that exact spot.

In my experience, and I spent many nights chasing elephants in the Duars, elephants generally entered the tea estates at night and left early in the morning. If, by any chance, they could not make it back in time, they usually spent the whole day stranded in one place on the estate. While this happened rarely, and once, I happened to have my camera with me and was able to take some photographs.

People have retaliated, and some elephants have been found shot and also poisoned. The problem persists, and no solution seems to be in sight.

While the above incident actually happened, it is not to be taken as the norm. The situation is terrible, and many deaths occur, but major incidents like this have never happened again.

However, elephants are comparatively very aggressive in the Duars, and when they charge, it is usually for real. The term mock charge does not exist in the Duars' vocabulary.

Often known as the spotted feline or the prince of cats, leopards are another animal, besides elephants, that comes into conflict with man in the Duars. Happily, however, without such drastic consequences.

One day, a Jeep pulled up in front of my bungalow with two gentlemen from the WWF who were monitoring leopard conflict in the area. They were out collecting information, and I seized the opportunity to familiarise myself with the issue. To my surprise, it was more widespread than I had imagined.

The main problem seemed to be what was misunderstood as 'abandoned cubs'. Leopards don't 'abandon' their cubs; they leave them in a safe place (often in one of the many drains that are abundant in the tea fields) when they go looking for prey. These 'rescued' cubs don't need rescuing — just leave them where you found them, and their mother will return for them. They also stressed on the availability of water during the dry season, as leopards would often enter the labour lines in search of water. They suggested we dig a few pits to store water in specific locations identified during their fieldwork.

I would like to point out that finding leopard cubs on the estate was quite a regular feature. Besides the drains, land in the estates had to be rehabilitated for two years after the old tea was uprooted.

Guatemala grass is planted as a rehabilitation crop, which grows to a height of six to seven feet. These areas were a haven for leopards, and every patch of Guatemala grass had its resident leopard or leopard family. They used to find it an ideal place to litter as the area would be undisturbed for two years.

I remember vividly the first leopard sighting for my daughter Tara. Realising my interest in wildlife, some of the workers told me to keep a lookout for leopards when the tea bushes start recovering from pruning. According to them, leopards liked to sit under such bushes in the evenings. I, like most people, dismissed their theory out of hand. This is a typical response when someone who you consider 'less educated' or 'less aware' than you come up with a theory. In my defence, I would like to state that I was still young.

I was now in the division that Rajan had previously managed, which was an 'out division', i.e. it was in a separate location quite far away from the main estate — in this case, about 20 km away. Late one evening, after dark, I was returning from the main estate office on my motorcycle when my headlights caught a leopard sitting by the side of the road just as I took a turn.

It was a typical narrow and winding estate field road, and before I could react, I had passed about three feet away from her. While she followed me with a look of curiosity in her eyes, she barely moved; she just turned her head to watch me. It could be my imagination, but I recall a look of amusement on her face.

As soon as I reached the bungalow, I quickly bundled Tara and Gowri into our Jeep and promptly drove out. Lucky for us, she was still there, sitting absolutely unconcerned, and we were able to observe her for a good twenty minutes. She finally got up, crossed the road, and disappeared into the tea field. Tara was less than a year old, and as you may have guessed, the leopard was sitting under tea recovering from pruning.

The Forest Department has a rehabilitation program, and problem animals are trapped and released into the many sanctuaries and national parks nearby. A special cage was used for trapping these leopards. The cage had two compartments, one larger than the other. The larger compartment had a trap door that was triggered by a tripwire pulled across it. A goat or a dog would be placed in the smaller compartment (as bait), and the cage would be placed where the target leopard had been last seen. The leopard could only get to the bait by entering the larger compartment. The leopard would trigger the tripwire while doing so and effectively lock itself into the cage. The bait was perfectly safe as there was no way the leopard could actually get to it — after a traumatic night, the bait (dog or goat) would be released, and the trapped leopard transferred to the rehab centre at Jaldapara.

There were some interesting incidents. Once, a manager had to protect a trapped leopard from a mob hell-bent on killing it by placing himself between the mob and the cage. He managed to hold his ground till the Forest Department officials came and took away the leopard. My friend Ashim was allowed to keep a cub he had found on the estate. He named her Leo and fostered her for six months. After handing her over he used to go and play with her in Jaldapara. She was eventually released in the Buxa Tiger Reserve.

A few years previously, a cub was found close to my division, and there was an opportunity to foster the cub for a few months. I was a bachelor at that time and shared accommodation with a married couple with two small children (it was a two-storied bungalow, and they occupied the top floor). Unfortunately, they objected vehemently to the idea.

Encounters with leopards were never as dramatic as those with elephants, but they had a charm of their own. Once, when returning with Gowri from a friend's place, we saw one having a drink from the hand pump in the army compound in Damdim.

One afternoon, a dead leopard was found in the area surrounding the Sylee manager's bungalow. It was a large male well past its prime, and its death seemed natural. Unfortunately, it was the workers who found it, and by the time the information reached us, they had hacked off its paws and made off with the claws. Because of that, we had quite a time dealing with the forest department people who suspect foul play because of the missing feet.

The only injury occurred one afternoon when, while we were conducting spraying operations, a leopard leapt out of the bushes and scrambled over one worker in an attempt to escape. Luckily, the worker's backpack machine bore the brunt, and he escaped with minor scratches. However, the man was very shaken up and had to be hospitalised. I guess a leopard springing on you can be quite traumatising.

I also remember one morning, my mother-in-law (who was visiting us) told me that she had seen two leopards from the guest room window. Sure enough, the next day, we saw their pugmarks all over our freshly ploughed kitchen garden. We had two dogs at that time and luckily for us the leopards never troubled them. I believe that wild animals can judge people and do not trouble people who they think don't pose any danger to them.

Stumbling upon the remains of leopard kills was also a frequent occurrence. These kills were mostly dogs and occasionally a young calf. Having read up a lot of wildlife, I would examine these kills carefully to look for the telltale signs of typical leopard feeding behaviour — like them starting to feed from the stomach rather than the hindquarters (tigers typically begin with the hindquarters). I never reported or made any unnecessary noise about these findings, as it would only attract adverse reactions. People generally had no idea of the extent of leopard activity in the estates, which was a good thing.

Gowri, Tara, and I used to visit Jaldapara and the rescue centre quite often as they were located very close to one of the estates that I was working on. We would spend some time with the leopards and have lunch at the tourist lodge before returning home.

We also visited the rescue centre at the Buxa Tiger Reserve, which, in addition to leopards, also had a few sloth bears and hog deer. Things were a bit more relaxed those days and we had easy access to the cages. Buxa was a fair distance away, and we weren't frequent visitors.

THE SOUND OF BAGPIPES

I have, for some reason, always been fascinated by the sound of the bagpipes. I have no idea where or how I acquired the taste. Maybe it was when my mother watched the Beating Retreat on television every year. She would often talk of being taken there as a child by her father. When I was studying in Delhi, I would often go to listen to the rehearsals. The bagpipes played by the army regiments were excellent.

When I visited my uncle, who was the Corp Commander in Sukna, he had arranged for two pipers to march into the Mess at the stroke of midnight to usher in the new year. It was one of my best new years' and in fact, I really do not remember any other as well as I remember that one. Unfortunately, I am not able to find any recordings of bagpipes in any of the music stores. It seems to be only played and taught by the Indian Army.

When I was posted in Sylee we had the Kumaon regiment as our neighbours. I would bunk work after breakfast and park outside the camp and spend an hour or two listening to their band practise the bagpipes. The soldiers later told me that the people of Kumaon and Gharwal had adopted the bagpipes and it has become an integral part of their culture, being played during important occasions. I was determined to visit but have not been able to do so. One day I will certainly go. It remains one of the things that needs to be done.

One day in Dalsingpara I had gone to the neighbouring basti to try and locate a tree that had been felled and stolen from the estate. As I was walking down the basti roads (a basti is a haphazard collection of agricultural fields and houses built in the centre of the holdings) I heard the sound of bagpipes! For a moment, I thought I was dreaming. However, there was no mistaking the sound. All thoughts of stolen trees were brushed aside as I tried to locate the piper. I managed to trace him and persuade him to come to my bungalow.

We spent an enjoyable afternoon listening to him play. His was a good story. He had been taught by an ex-army sergeant and was able to play all the old regimental tunes.

I have not had the good fortune of listening to live bagpipes since then.

RIVERS RUN THROUGH IT

If there is a common thread that runs unbroken through the later part of my life, it has to be rivers. This is in stark contrast to the early part of my life when sand dominated. While I was never drawn towards rivers, they turned out to be places I would turn to escape. Wastelands, scrub forests, grasslands, and open plains are what I enjoy the most, but rivers, hills and forests dominate my life now.

In many of the places where I have lived, my home was close to rivers, and we would go to the banks as a family to spend time together. The rivers of the Duars were placid streams during winter and raging torrents during the monsoon, often flooding their banks and causing a lot of damage. I learned very quickly that one cannot take them for granted.

As the cold weather offered us a lot of free time, it was then that we would go to the river for a swim or a picnic. During the monsoon, we would do our best to avoid them.

The rivers in the Duars remained clear most of the time, and one could see their rocky bottoms. The colours of the stones were beautiful, and we started a small collection. My daughter Tara loved rivers and would disappear on many afternoons to play in them. She was quite the waterbaby then.

My wife Gowri introduced me to fishing, and we would spend a lot of time indulging in the sport. Tara had her own little rod, and the entire family would have tremendous fun.

Gowri's tales of camping in the forests on the banks of the Cauvery fascinated me, and I was determined to do the same. The first step was to get hold of some equipment, which was easier than I had thought. We simply helped ourselves to the stock at her house and gradually managed to acquire some fantastic equipment. Our collection now includes the rods used by her grandfather and uncle.

Her uncle Chippy Briggs held the record for the largest mahseer caught. After that, we went to the rivers. Gowri taught me the rudiments of casting, and I soon became good enough to start fishing on my own. We always went fishing as a family, and Tara also took to it. We fished in some of the great rivers of the Duars, namely the Toorsa, the Jaldhaka and the Chel. Unfortunately, we were not able to make it to the Teesta.

We would get up early in the morning for the Jaldhaka as it was a fair distance from the bungalow I lived in then, but most of the time, we would go to Toorsa in the evenings, which was just behind us. We would drive down to the river in our vehicle. First, I had a Jeep, then a Gypsy and finally a Sierra. The Sierra was painted to blend into the dry riverbed of the Toorsa. Driving on the dry riverbed was one of the highlights of our trips.

Since then we have restricted our fishing trips to the Kabini. However the Kabini is too crowded with nets, and it is usually too windy to cast correctly. The Kabini is also, most of the time, a lake and not a river. Man has shackled the Kabini and condemned it to a lifetime of slavery.

The Kabini River now dominates my life, and though it is extremely beautiful, it somehow lacks the character of the rivers of the Duars. The rivers of the Duars run wild; no dams block their path, and I hope they remain that way — forever free.

BACK TO THE BASICS

My photographic journey started in the 1970s when my father presented me with an Agfa Click 3 camera. I used this camera to take my first wildlife photograph of a tusker in Bandipur. From there, I progressed through many upgrades and acquired my first SLR camera in the 1990s.

Kabini offered me the perfect opportunity to practise and hone my skills, and this very same SLR with a 70 – 210 mm lens was my workhorse for the first few years. I then moved on to video and finally to digital with a point-and-shoot.

Sometime in 2007 I found myself without a camera and at this critical juncture, my mother-in-law stepped in and presented me with her brother's old camera. It was a totally manual Fujica SLR film camera with a selection of some very good lenses—28 mm, 55 mm, and 300 mm. This was a bonanza as far as I was concerned, and it offered me an opportunity to return to the drawing board and test my skills anew.

After shooting a few rolls in colour, I decided to truly return to my roots and shoot in black and white. The biggest hurdles were finding film and people who still processed B&W. Much to my delight and surprise, this was not as big a hurdle as I had anticipated, as I found out that GG Welling on MG Road still processed film.

The only issue I faced was with regard to the choice of film. The only 35 mm B&W film I could get my hands on had a rated speed of 100 ASA, which was not ideally suited to wildlife photography. The logistics were another factor, as I had to send the exposed film to Bangalore to get it processed. I also had to scan the prints to be able to share them on the then-nascent social media platforms. Unfortunately the quality of the scan was not great while the prints looked much better.

The exposure settings were done entirely by experience and no metering system whatsoever was employed, as the exposure meter was not in a working condition. The focusing was also manual and handheld without any image stabilisation. To top it all off, the 300 mm lens mount was defective, leading to many focus issues. With time, I was able to 'read' it properly and achieve focus.

Improvisation was the name of the game, and I had to keep tightening the screws on the lens. I carried a pocket knife with me to do so, and my guests would have a good laugh whenever I pulled it out and started making adjustments to the 300 mm lens. At one point in time, fed up with the constant battle with the 300 mm, I shot exclusively with the 28 and 55 mm lenses.

The biggest coincidence was my meeting with TNA Perumal (the veteran wildlife photographer who has done a lot of work in black and white). However, I was too hesitant to show him my work.

This phase gave me maximum pleasure and satisfaction and taught me, all over again, the virtue of patience.

THE MYSTIC NATURALIST

I have often been asked why I left Kabini and moved to Bangalore. What was it that made me leave (what many saw as) my 'dream job' – why one would ever dream of working is a question best left for another day.

As the years rolled on, I became rather disillusioned with the creeping commercialisation of the destination. Kabini was becoming a popular holiday spot in contrast to being a truly wildlife one and this slowly made it lose its charm for me. The wildlife experience was being commoditised so that it could be neatly packaged and sold to a new clientele.

The role of a Naturalist was also undergoing a fundamental change, one that I was not comfortable with. I found myself increasingly delegating safari duties to my colleagues and only accompanying people

I knew previously or those referred by them. After a while, matters came to a head, and I had to admit that I was no longer enjoying myself.

This was an unpleasant realisation for me as I had forged a deep connection with the natural world, and acknowledging that it was in danger of being broken was no easy task. I came to the reluctant and ugly conclusion that in order to preserve my connection with the wild I had to take a break – to sever all connections for as long as needed.

Once I left Kabini and settled into a different lifestyle, I often wondered about the changes that may have occurred and how people today perceive a Naturalist. What does the term even stand for now?

The word 'Naturalist' is much bandied about these days and at first it was used to describe a person who made a living guiding visitors into a National Park or Wildlife Sanctuary but has since been appropriated by a host of people. It is now widely used by a large cross-section of people who have an interest in and knowledge of natural history. Many of them do not necessarily make a living out of it.

While a lot of such people use the term to describe themselves there is a section that does not do the same. These are the members of the scientific community who have a formal education in natural history. They prefer to draw a distinction between themselves and the professional Naturalist – there is an element of implied superiority.

So the question arises: What or who is a Naturalist? Is a scientist not a Naturalist? I decided to tackle the question by using a method we used to understand words and terms in school: I referred to two sources, one a classical dictionary and the other a contemporary online source. Given below are the definitions that I found . . .

As per the Merriam-Webster dictionary

1. A student of natural history especially: a field biologist
   As per Vocabulary.com

1. A biologist knowledgeable about natural history (especially botany and zoology)
2. An advocate of the doctrine that the world can be understood in scientific terms

As mentioned earlier, in India, the term was initially used to describe a particular set of professionals who made a living by guiding guests in our National Parks and Wildlife Sanctuaries. Such professionals were generally English speakers with a college education, hailing primarily from an urban background as opposed to the 'Guide' who spoke in his mother tongue, did not have much formal education and lived in villages adjacent to the National Park/Sanctuary where he worked. The former, as did the latter, had a great love and passion for the outdoors and made a conscious decision, despite pressure from their families, to do what they did.

Over time, with the advent of the digital revolution in India and the subsequent rise in disposable incomes, National Parks and Wildlife Sanctuaries became extremely popular destinations. The term Naturalist began to be slowly appropriated by the 'wildlife enthusiast', a person who regularly visited National Parks, for the lack of a better word, as a tourist. He was not a professional Naturalist per se (he earned his living in another industry) but shared many of the other traits of his professional counterparts.

Eventually this increase in tourist inflow and business led to an increased demand for the "professionalisation" of the Naturalist's role. What was basically a network dominated by lodges run by the Forest Department, and a few standalone units run by people with a genuine interest in wildlife, quickly became an industry. It was propelled further by the arrival of some of the bigger players in the Indian travel and tourism league and their overseas partners.

These industry experts brought with them, among other things, good and bad, their own notions of professionalism and associated training methods. This led to the rise of a new definition of the

Naturalist. He was now a trained or professional Naturalist – a person who had undergone a formal training program run by one of these organisations with expert trainers courtesy of their overseas partners. These trained Naturalists were also drawn, more or less, from the same social strata as the original Naturalists. The only difference was that now a certification had suddenly become vital; apparently, without it, one could not be called a Naturalist.

Many people consider a Naturalist's training program an excellent idea, one that can produce individuals with a certain standard of knowledge and set of skills that are necessary for the industry. A formal, recognised training system is a huge asset in meeting the minimum requirement, but such systems can and do suffer from huge lacuna.

While I would not like to tar everyone with the same brush, in my experience, some of the major failings of any such system is that they have the tendency to degenerate into assembly lines, churning out a long line of 'cookie cutter' professionals with the same philosophy and outlook. No doubt there is a good foundation in terms of knowledge and skills, but such a system fails owing to its reliance on what I would call formal education or the scientific thought process. It restricts one to knowledge that is accessible purely by the intellect.

Another change that this professionalisation brought about was in the recruitment process. The recruitment of professional Naturalists by new businesses was conducted by their various Human Resources departments, which started, as is their wont, preferring people with degrees in related fields such as ecology and forestry. This is a common practice across all industries, possibly another consequence of the 'trained' mind.

In the past people chose such professions because they felt a profound connection with the natural world. A connection that opened them to symbolic or spiritual interpretation and led to knowledge inaccessible by the intellect – learnings that can only be attained through contemplation and self-surrender.

Now, before you start wondering, let me reiterate the acknowledged fact that human perception is limited by the senses. Our hearing is limited, we cannot see in the dark, our sense of smell is not acute, and so on – in short, there is an entire universe out there that is beyond our intellectual and sensory comprehension. And yet we restrict ourselves to that which only the intellect can perceive, willingly ignoring the strongest of our facilities – our imagination.

In my opinion, most modern-day Naturalists do not transcend the professional boundaries imposed upon them by their profession. He lacks a deep reverence for the natural world or an appreciation of its complexity.

I noticed this change slowly creeping into the profession as the years went by, and that's when I decided to step out to protect what was left of my natural curiosity. Previously, while conducting a safari, my attention used to be focused on the forest – looking for signs, listening for calls, and soaking in the sounds and smells of the wild. By the end of my career, it was focused more on the people in the Jeep – on keeping them 'engaged' with scripted storytelling et al.

Patience has transformative powers beyond compare, and in today's world of instant gratification, it is conspicuous by its absence. Patience is the key to mindful observation, which in turn leads to meaningful connections with the natural world. An appreciation of the silence and solitude of the wild, emotional intelligence, empathy, and a deeper appreciation for the present moment cannot be taught – they must be acquired. The Mystic Naturalist must possess all of those traits.

I use the term Mystic Naturalist to describe those with a philosophical and spiritual bent of mind, those who acknowledge the fact that to develop a deep connection with the natural world, one must be prepared to go beyond the boundaries imposed by conventional wisdom. They must embrace the innate wisdom of the 'primitive' self and reignite the curiosity of their childhood days to become seekers once again.

Groundbreaking ideas come neither from the centre nor from peer reviews. They are born in the silence at the edge of the abyss. Would a candlemaker ever think of inventing the light bulb?

A Mystic, to my understanding, is one who seeks unity with or absorption into the divine or the absolute and who believes in the spiritual apprehension of truths that are beyond the intellect.

The Mystic Naturalist, therefore, seeks unity with the natural world through contemplation and self-surrender, pushing the envelope by seeking truths far beyond the reach of the intellect. Such a being realises that he is not separate from the natural world but an integral part of it. He acknowledges that this connection had been broken years ago and endeavours to reunite with it.

I like to believe that I belong to the family of Mystic Naturalists and so find myself a pronounced misfit in the world of trained professionals.

ABOUT THE AUTHOR

Vikram Nanjappa likes to be described as an interested and well-informed amateur. He draws inspiration from the band of men called the Orientalists, most of whom were amateurs. Like them, his field of enquiry is 'Man and Nature; (with an emphasis on Nature) whatever is performed by the one or produced by the other'.

Vikram's first exposure to wildlife came through the shikar tales he had heard from his friends while studying at Mayo College in Ajmer in Rajasthan, one of the country's oldest and celebrated institutions of learning. Vikram cites the writings of Billy Arjan Singh and Jim Corbett as having played a pivotal role in inclining him passionately and committedly towards wildlife.

After completing his Bachelor's in History and Political Science from St. Stephen's College in New Delhi, Vikram joined the tea plantations. It was during the thirteen years he spent in Kerala and the Duars of West Bengal that he found the opportunity to hone his twin hobbies of wildlife and photography. In 2002 he moved to Kabini and took up organising wildlife tours full time. He is one of those rare gems who managed to turn his passion into a rewarding and fulfilling vocation.

After leaving Kabini, in a manner of natural progression, Vikram ventured into the field of wildlife conservation (Non-profit Organization Management) with the Asian Nature Conservation

Foundation for a few years. He also explored the world of fashion as a freelance writer and as a photographer. His current avatar is that of a marketing professional.

Vikram avers that traditional knowledge and field skills coupled with good science and common sense is the best way to understand, expose and preserve our wildlife, which is alarmingly on the decline. He strongly disapproves of what he calls the 'tabloid portrayal' of wildlife, where aberrant animal behaviour is highlighted to reinforce false myths and stereotypes. This has to be eclipsed by an attitude of respect and reverence for the animal kingdom if we are to continue enjoying sightings of our wild brethren in their natural habitats.

Currently residing in Bangalore, Vikram works with Evolve Back Resorts as a marketing maestro.